Orchestrating the Power of Groups:
Beginnings, Middles, and Endings
(overture, movements, and finales)

Proceedings of the XXVIII Annual International Symposium
of the Association for the Advancement of Social Work with Groups

Orchestrating the Power of Groups
Beginnings, Middles, and Endings
(overture, movements, and finales)

Edited by

Dominique Moyse Steinberg

w&b

MMX

© Whiting & Birch Ltd 2010
Published by Whiting & Birch Ltd,
Forest Hill, London SE23 3HZ

ISBN 9781861771278

Printed in England and the United States by Lightning Source

Contents

Acknowledgements

Association for the Advancement of Social Work with Groups, Inc.
XXVIII Annual International Symposium
San Diego, October 12-15, 2006

We thank the following for their hard work and support
which contributed to making the XXVIII Anniversary
Symposium of AASWG a success:

Symposium Co-Chairs
Helen E. Antoniak and Albert E. Schafer

The San Diego Planning Committee
Sonia and Paul Abels

Kurt Buske

Velma Carrio

Jeanne Gill

Anne Kopp-Hyman

Jane Hynes

Ruth Howell

Emil Jech

Cheryl Lee

Gary McKay

Joan Parry

JoAnn Regan

Mary Ann and David Pollack

Maricela Perla Rodriguez

Adylin Rosenblatt

Judith Schieberl

Joan Schomburg

Steven Sherber

About the Editor

Dominique Moyse Steinberg, DSW is on faculty of Hunter College School of Social Work in New York City, USA, where she teaches social group work, social work research methods, and professional writing. She is the author of *A Mutual-Aid Approach to Working with Groups* (2nd ed.) and *The Social Work Student's Research Companion*, both published by Taylor & Francis/Routledge, and has written extensively about the role of mutual aid in social group work. With special emphasis on training social workers to deal with group conflict, she has presented regularly at the annual symposia of the Association for the Advancement of Social Work with Groups. She has been a member of the Association since 1983 and currently serves on its Executive Committee. Steinberg is an editorial board member of *Social Work with Groups* and *Journal of Teaching in Social Work*.

The contributors

Robert Basso, PhD. RSW is Associate Professor at the Faculty of Social Work, Wilfrid Laurier University in Waterloo Ontario. He teaches Introductory and Advanced Group Work in the MSW program. His interest include children's groups, and teen mental health groups. He currently is the Chair of the University Research Ethics Board.

Shantih E. Clemans, DSW is on faculty at Wurzweiler School of Social Work, Yeshiva University, in New York City, where she teaches Group Work, Foundations of Social Work, among other courses. A former Chair of the New York City Red Apple Chapter of AASWG, Shantih specializes in group work, secondary trauma, teaching methodologies, and feminist research approaches.

Mark Doel is Professor Emeritus at Sheffield Hallam University, England. He graduated from Oxford and qualified as a social worker in 1974. He has almost twenty years of social work practice experience during which he specialised in groupwork. Mark is widely published, with 16 books to his name, seven in foreign translations, and numerous peer-reviewed articles. He was co-editor of *Groupwork* journal and is founder editor of the *Journal of Social Policy and Social Work in Transition*.

Anna S. Fritz, MSSA was a former faculty member of the Mandel School of Applied Social Sciences at Case Western Reserve University where she taught group work. She was also actively involved in the Executive Committee of Northeast Ohio Chapter of the AASWG and was Chair of the Education Committee.

Alex Gitterman, EdD is the Zachs Professor of Social Work and Director of the Doctoral Program at the University of Connecticut School of Social Work. Alex has co-edited: *Mental health and social problems: A social work perspective* (2010); *The encyclopedia of social work with groups* (2009); and *Mutual aid, vulnerable and resilient populations, and the life cycle.* He has also authored *The Life Model of social work practice: Advances in theory and practice,* Third Edition (2008); and *The handbook of social work practice with vulnerable and resilient populations*, Second Edition, (2001).

Urania Glassman, MA, MSW, DSW, LCSW has been Director of Field Instruction, Wurzweiler School of Social Work Yeshiva University since 1993. She has written and presented on group work and on field education for three decades. Her recent volume *Group Work: A Humanistic and Skills Building Approach*, 2nd Edition, was published in 2008 by Sage. She serves on the CSWE Commission on Educational Policy, co-chairs the Field Education Track, and NANFED – North American Network of Field Educators and Directors, and maintains a private practice.

Vicki Hallas, LCSW completed her MSW degree specializing in group work methodology from Hunter College School of Social Work where she studied under the tutelage of Dr. Roselle Kurland. Vicki is the Clinical Director of Counseling and Psychological Services at the College of Mount Saint Vincent in Riverdale, New York State. She hopes to implement technology-based, distance counseling for her center.

Karen Horn is a school social worker for Milwaukee Public Schools focusing on district-wide initiatives in Restorative Practices, RtI and Family Involvement. She is a member of the Positive Behavioral Supports and Interventions Advisory Committee for the State of Wisconsin. Karen completed her MSW at Loyola University in Chicago.

Timothy B. Kelly, PhD is Professor of Social Work, University of Dundee, School of Education, Social Work and Community Education, Dundee, Scotland. He is currently Co-Editor of *Groupwork* and writes in the areas of groupwork and older people. Before moving to Scotland in 2003 he taught at Barry University School of Social Work In Miami Shores, where he was an active member of the Beulah Rothman Center for Groupwork Studies. He was previously the Secretary and Vice-President of AASWG.

Cheryl D. Lee, PhD, MSW is Associate Professor, School of Social Work, California State University, Long Beach. She is Chair of the California Chapter of AASWG. Her research areas include: mentoring, group work, and policy and practice research to improve the well-being of at risk populations.

Susan E Mason, PhD is professor of social work and sociology at the Wurzweiler School of Social Work, Yeshiva University in New York. Her interests include evidence-based mental health interventions in groups and group centered research. She has written extensively on adolescent and young adult mental health treatment.

Ellen Sue Mesbur, MSW, EdD is Director and Professor at the School of Social Work, Renison University College, University of Waterloo, where she teaches social work with groups and field education. She has published in the areas of: the history of social group work in Canada; teaching and learning within the context of a small group; on-line teaching; and field education.

Eliette del Carmen Montiel, MSW is a psychiatric social worker at Los Angeles County Department of Mental Health. She is also the secretary of the AASWG California Chapter.

Kim Orchard is Deputy Manager of The Park (South Gloucestershire Children and Adolescent Services)

Dr. William Pelech, PhD, MSW, RSW is an Associate Professor at the Faculty of Social Work, University of Calgary. He has over 20 years of experience in group work related clinical research, education and practice. His book, *Dancing Towards Wholeness: Interpersonal Coordination in a Treatment Group* (2010) and related publications examine changing patterns of non-verbal behaviour over the life of a treatment group. He continues to practice and conduct research into group work in the Calgary area and has been co-principal investigator on a major grant relating to intergenerational trauma as well as an evaluative project that examined the impact of a community-based group mediation program upon the restoration of relationships between offenders and victims. He is also currently responsible for a major research project funded by the Alberta Centre for Child, Family and Community Research which evaluates the impact of enhanced practice standards for children who experience FASD.

Shirley R. Simon, MSW, ACSW, LCSW is Assistant Professor, School of Social Work, Loyola University Chicago, where she chairs the Group Work Practice Committee. She has been a social work educator for over thirty years, has published on group work education and history, and has facilitated over fifty student and recent alumni presentations at professional association conferences.

Thelma Silver, PhD, LISW-S is Associate Professor in the Department of Social Work Youngstown State University, where she has taught group work. She is currently Co-Chair of the Education Committee of Northeast Ohio chapter of the AASWG.

Joyce A. Webster, MSW, LCSW is a consultant for Jewish Child and Family Services in Chicago, where she trains students, clinicians and clinical supervisors. She served as Co-Chair of the XXXI Annual AASWG Symposium hosted in Chicago in 2009. Joyce is an alumna of the School of Social Work at Loyola University Chicago.

Introduction

Tuning in and Orchestrating the Power of Groups: Beginnings, Middles, and Endings (overture, movements, and finales)

It is a great pleasure to present to you the proceedings of the XXVIII Annual International Symposium of the Association for the Advancement of Social Work with Groups, held in San Diego, California, USA. Not only am I delighted that we have a set of proceedings for this exciting symposium, but as the daughter of a very musical family, the theme of this symposium and thus this edition particularly touches my heart.

It is really no surprise, although it took me some years to realize it (as I note in *The Magic of Mutual Aid, Social Work with Groups*, 25[1/2], 31-38) that I was drawn to group work as one of my two social work majors at the Hunter College School of Social Work. From my very first appearance on this earth I have been in, of, and surrounded by musical groups. From my very first days, therefore, I have witnessed both the value of conformity (yes, conformity) and the importance of individuality. Is that possible? Can both conformity and individuality co-exist in and even contribute to the same package? Of course! It is a fundamental principle of all ensemble work, be it musical or drama or social group work. Thus, I have always understood the importance for each musician in a quartet to be at the very least tuned to the same key, to work from a common score, to be on the same page, and to be at precisely the same moment in any given measure. At the same time, I have understood that when the musicians are at the same measure, each score has slightly different handwritten notations to guide the dynamics, and each instrument has a different sound to make and note to play. Without this individualization, the collective cannot be a true ensemble, and if the ensemble does not exist, music cannot take place. Conformity and individuality -- at the heart of music and also at the heart of social work practice with groups: on one hand common ground and common purpose and on the other, individual strength, individual ways of contributing, and individual ways of making meaning. To transform another metaphor in the service of rendering this point, there are many roads to Rome, but everyone must agree that Rome is the place to meet!

It is a very special pleasure, therefore, to bring you 11 papers that speak in one way or other to the musical theme of this symposium, *Orchestrating the Power of Groups*, be it by reminding us of the fundamental values of social group work or by identifying the various processes that make this professional social work method so powerful and artistic a helping medium.

Overture/Beginnings

As with all beginnings we set the stage with *Mutual Aid: Back to Basics*, by Alex Gitterman. In this opening chapter, Gitterman reminds us why we practice as we do and laments the increasing ignorance or manipulation of process in much work with groups in today's social-control sound-byte world, a world into which social work practice has been heftily co-opted. The next three chapters speak in particular to the tuning in and beginnings of professionalization – that is, to the role of education in promoting ethical and effective social work practice with groups. In Chapter 2 (*Orchestrating the Power of a Group of AASWG Members in Partnership for Change with Colleagues at an University Social Work Program*) Thelma Silver and Anna Fritz (deceased) describe a collaboration between AASWG and an educational institution that was successful in at least one instance of stemming the very tide of which Gitterman speaks. Chapter 3 (*Mentoring in Groups*) by Cheryl Lee and Eliette del Carmen Montiel takes the discussion of collaborative power to the more intimate plane of group mentoring in educational institutions, proposing the use of formal group-mentoring structures as an effective strategy for promoting professional success. Ellen-Sue Mesbur returns the discussion to the broader stage with *A Magical Mystery Tour: Education and Social Work with Groups across Borders*, through which she eloquently demonstrates the potential of cross-cultural exchange to strengthen education as well as practice.

Middles/Movements

The discussion then turns to practice, research, and contemporary issues beginning with Chapter 5, *The Facilitator 411 on Phone Groups: When Caller ID Isn't Enough*, by Vicki Hallas. Hallas discusses one of the growing challenges of modern-day group work in the use of technology to facilitate a support group, using a case example to illustrate in particular the struggle of applying traditional visual-based skills to auditory practice. In the next chapter (*Groupwork Researchers as "Temporary Insiders"*) Mark Doel and Kim Orchard propose an approach to, offer a case example of, and discuss the implications of an approach to participant observation in which independent evaluation is conducted by a person external to the group. In Chapter 7 (*Dancing Towards Wholeness: The Impact of Conflict on Patterns of Interpersonal Coordination in a Small Treatment Group*) William Pelech and Robert Basso turn our attention to the study of a more specific aspect of group work: the use of cluster analysis to examine the influence of conflict on a group's capacity for interpersonal coordination. Tim Kelly, Debbie Tolson, Tracy Day Smith, and Gillian McColgan then describe in Chapter 8 (*Using the Research Process to Develop Group Services for Older Persons with a Hearing Disability*) the use of a mixed-methods study as a needs assessment for designing practice that will help older people to successfully adjust to life with a hearing aid. Concluding this area of focus with Chapter 9, Shantih Clemans and Susan Mason bring our attention to the utility of combining evidence-based group work (clinical practice) with a particular research approach (participatory action research) in *Participatory Research and Evidence-based Practice for Rape Survivor Groups: Implications for Practice and Teaching*. In this chapter Clemans and Mason suggest that groups envisioned, planned, and formed in a participatory format can contribute to practice that is clinically relevant and useful and propose a model of practice that combines evidence-based strategies with a participatory research framework.

Endings/Finales

This last section returns the discussion to the broad stage of human rights and the future of group work. In Chapter 10 (*Relevance of Group*

Work's Humanistic Values and Democratic Norms To Contemporary Global Crises, Urania Glassman proposes that the humanistic values of group work and the democratic norms that they operationalize are both in concert with human rights as identified by the United Nations and provide a value base and benchmark for developing democratic-participation skills and interactional skills for bridging cultural barriers. Finally, the last chapter by Shirley Simon, Joyce Webster, and Karen Horn (*A Critical Call for Connecting Students and Professional Associations*) ties together the call for applying group work norms and values to the global stage with the earlier call for formal group mentorship by calling for greater conscious effort to advance and strengthen our emerging leadership.

Beginnings ... Middles ... Endings. Overture ... Movements ... Finale. I think you will agree that this set of proceedings takes on in parallel form the theme of the symposium it represents beginning with education, moving into the "work details" of practice and research, and ending with reflections on the potential of group work in the larger profession and global scenes. I hope you will also agree that whichever the metaphor, the discussion contained in this volume realizes both the harmony and modulation required to advance meaningful production, be it music or group work.

Acknowledgements

Many thanks to my colleagues for graciously submitting their work to peer review for consideration as a chapter in this set of proceedings. Thanks as well to the reviewers for devoting time, energy, and editorial feedback in putting this volume together. Finally, thanks to David Whiting of Whiting & Birch for his more than gracious support in both developing and delivering this *Proceedings of the XXVIII Annual International Symposium of the Association for the Advancement of Social Work with Groups*.

Dr. Dominique Moyse Steinberg

1
Mutual aid: Back to basics

Alex Gitterman

Summary

The current practice of group work is almost unrecognizable to those of us who were professionally raised in the social goals traditions. A typical group led by a group worker used to be rich in group process. In contemporary practice, group process is ignored, controlled and/or manipulated rather than trusted. The group primarily serves as a context, as a backdrop for the dissemination of information aimed at changing people's behaviors, perceptions and thinking. Trusting, having faith in, and cherishing mutual aid and group process have become alien notions. The paper describes how this sad state of affairs came to be.

Introduction

The current practice of group work is almost unrecognizable to those of us who were professionally raised in the social goals traditions (Coyle, 1947, 1948; Klein, 1953; Wilson & Ryland, 1949). What ever happened to the group as a cornerstone for a democratic citizenry? What ever happened to the group as the medium for the traversing of developmental tasks and acquisition of developmental skills? What ever happened to the group composed of people in the same boat helping each other to 'navigate the stormy waters of life?' What ever happened to the group as the primary agent for social change, or a more basic question: Whatever happened to the group as a group in the provision of group work services?

A typical group led by a group worker used to be rich in group process. Consider the following: A hospital social worker had invited eight cardiac patients to form a group. We join them in the first meeting after refreshments and introductions (Gitterman & Germain, 2008, pp. 170-173):

> After the refreshments and introductions, I said, As I had explained to each one of you individually, you were invited to participate in a four-session group for patients with recent heart attacks. The staff believed you could be helpful to one another in dealing with your concerns about hospitalization, the heart attack, and what the future has in store for you.
>
> Bill indicated that work worries him the most. Mario, Hector, and John agreed. In an agitated way, Bill continued, If the doctor won't let me go back to work, what can I do? It has been twenty-seven years of my life and I always put in an honest day. Now the doctor says give it up. What kind of bullshit is that? Doesn't he realize that I have family and financial obligations? Lenny agreed, stating angrily that the doctors don't care that a medical recommendation could destroy a man's life.
>
> I asked if they were mostly annoyed about what their doctors said, or how they said it, or both? Hector explained that he thought it was a doctor's responsibility to make work recommendations in order to protect health, no matter the economic consequences. He has ended up on welfare and that's been hard to swallow. Bill responded with intensity that no doctor was ever going to do that to him, and he released a barrage of angry words. Mario suggested that Bill was doing what he himself has stopped doing—taking out the anger at the doctor's recommendation on his own heart. Hector understood Bill's being fighting mad because he, too, is having a hell of a time living with his 'bum ticker.' He is just beginning to calm down and to realize that it will never be the same. Bill shook his head in disbelief, How can I be calm? I have a family to take care of. Lenny explained that he also has a family, but getting excited and upset will only lead to another heart attack. Andy supported Bill. Peter exclaimed, But, shit, common sense will tell a man that health is the only important thing and everything else has to become second.

Most members agreed that if they let themselves get excited or experience too much pressure, they will only hurt themselves. Bill became angry again, telling group members that they had to be as dumb as the doctors to be forgetting their problems. Bill's eyes teared as he shouted, If the doctor says give up truck driving where I feel like a real man, what am I going to turn to? Who is going to hire me? What good am I? Lenny suggested that Bill calm down. Mario suggested that Bill talk to his boss and ask about a light job. Bill was insulted by the suggestions and shouted that he has pride and isn't going to degrade himself and tell the boss to pity him, to give him crumbs. What kind of man did Mario think he is, anyway? Mario answered, I think you are a good man and I respect you. I know a wounded animal has to fight for his brood, but Bill you have brains; you have to listen to your body and accept its limits. It takes a man to talk to his boss about lighter work.

I said that it seemed some of them have made peace with their hearts, while others are still fighting. Either way, I realize how much pain they are experiencing. Peter implored Bill to take it easy, to accept his heart condition. Bill insisted that his boss wouldn't give him light work because it would raise insurance rates. He feels he is no longer a man. At this point, Bill began to sob. Several members tried to change the subject, but I encouraged others to share their struggles. Walter referred to the mortgage and his family food needs. Hector talked of his pension and how it helps. In a disgusted tone, Bill wanted to know how he was going to get by with workers' compensation.

Mario spoke quietly but firmly: Bill, I can see you are a big man, strong, and you can beat anybody here in a fight, but I'm gonna tell you something, you gotta stop crying and be a real man. That means accept what is, do what has to be done, face the facts. You want to help your family, you ain't gonna help them by killing yourself. You have to cut down on your expectations, do what the doctors say, and start to build a new life.

Everyone waited for Bill's reaction. He stared at Mario as if trying to decide what to do. After a while, he said, I guess I could sell my home and buy a smaller one. My oldest son can go to work. Peter put his hand on Bill's back, saying that it was much better to be a live father than a dead one. Hector agreed, suggesting that they are all afraid of the same thing but handle it differently. Each man then spoke of how they changed or plan to change life styles and habits, and of their fears and common objective: 'Life!' Bill said the guys had been helpful. He continued, I'm a man, and I'll do what has to be done.

For another example, a social worker was struck by how the psychiatric hospital environment reinforced a sense of helplessness among an inpatient group of depressed members. Hospital research staff regularly recruited patients for research protocols: at a time convenient to the staff and often inconvenient for the patients. Patients were given no prior notice regarding the type or timing of the testing. The lack of prior notice created anxiety and inconveniences for the patients. The social worker thought members could help each other with this common experience in learning to deal with the demands of the outside world (Gitterman & Germain, 2008, pp 374-376.)

Mrs. King:	(rushing into the room out of breath and exasperated): I'm sorry I'm late; the research people asked me if I would be willing to take more tests, so I was upstairs - AGAIN!
Mrs. Simmons:	They really upset me. Last Friday - Good Friday - actually it ended up being BAD FRIDAY - those research people asked me to do a few studies. They kept me over two hours. In the meantime, my friend Gloria came to accompany me to Good Friday Mass. I can't get out of this place without a chaperone. She left after an hour and I missed Mass.
Social Worker:	Ouch - is this testing mandatory?
Mrs. King:	Well, it helps them with research that might help someone else someday.
Social Worker:	How is it actually helping you?
Mrs. Thomas:	It isn't helping me, it's just easier to go along with it than put up a stink.
Social Worker:	Mrs. King, is that the way you also experience it?
Mrs. King:	Yes.
Mrs. Martin:	Well, I don't think we should go along with it!
Social Worker:	Okay — how could you respond differently to them?
Mrs. Martin:	Oh, gosh, I don't know, but we shouldn't let people

	test us if we don't want to.
Mrs. Frankos:	I can't even say 'no' to my two year old, how am I going to say 'no' to a doctor?
Mrs. Simmons:	You too? Wait until they're fifteen and you still can't refuse them!
Social Worker:	I think we have a theme song, ladies: I'm a Girl Who Can't Say No! (We all laughed and Mrs. Martin went on to complete the second line) I'm in a terrible fix.

Using an assertiveness behavior sequence (1. Describe behavior; 2. Express associated feelings; 3. Request specified change; and 4. Identify positive consequences), the social worker helped members to complain effectively. Group members, by and large, demonstrated significant improvement in their communication skills. Mrs. King, however, continued to find it difficult. After four more sessions, Mrs. King once again raised a concern about resuming therapy with her psychiatrist.

Mrs. King:	I'm a little afraid of my contact with my doctor. I know so much more now about my illness and my medication thanks to you helping me ask the questions. I don't agree with the way he prescribes new medication, a hundred pills at a time. Then if I have any side effects and we have to change the medication I have all these pills left and wasted money.
Mrs. Simmons:	Why don't you just ask him to prescribe smaller doses?
Mrs. Tomas:	He'd probably tell her he was the doctor and knew best.
Social Worker:	Is that how you think he would respond? (Mrs. King was unsure what the doctor would say.) How do you think you might approach him about this?
Mrs. King:	Well, I'd tell him (she looked down) No. I'd ask him (she looked at me and smiled) No ... I'd tell him (looking down again) I'd rather you give me fewer

	pills at one time so if they had side effects it won't end up costing me so much money.
Social Worker:	Could you close your eyes and visualize your doctor's office — how he would look, and how you would feel saying those words to him?
Mrs. King:	(She looked down for a long time silently, then looked up) Please rewrite the prescription with fewer pills so if they have side effects it won't end up costing me so much money. (Everyone applauded and laughed, Mrs. Simmons congratulated her, and Mrs. Martin began to sing, We're Just the Girls who CAN Say No...)

In my teaching, faculty, field advising, staff development seminars and consultations, this type of raw mutual aid in these practice vignettes is rarely evident in contemporary practice. I rarely see a student or worker go with the flow and trust the group process. What I observe instead are social work students and workers ignoring, controlling and/or manipulating the group process. To them, the group primarily serves as a context, as a backdrop for the dissemination of information aimed at changing people's behaviors, perceptions and thinking. Trusting, having faith in, and cherishing mutual aid and group process have become alien notions. How did this come to be?

I believe that managed care's emphasis on cost reduction and cost containment has had a profound impact on the practice (as well as education) of social work with groups. Social agencies are under intense external pressure to demonstrate the efficacy of programs and interventions. To managed care, putting people in groups seems like an economically efficient method of providing services. In order to demonstrate the efficacy of group interventions, the profession has been forced to turn inward, toward a narrow focus on evaluating and demonstrating the effectiveness of professional interventions in inducing individual change - whether it be changing thinking processes, or managing one's anger, or learning parenting skills.

This turn inward has been at the expense of social group work's historical commitment to transactional definitions of life circumstances, events and stressors and to environmental interventions. Focusing on narrow, measurable individual behavioral changes ignores the struggles for survival and complexities of life in groups composed of oppressed members.

Schön poignantly recognizes the distortion created by removing the people from their social context:

> In the varied topography of professional practice, there is a high ground overlooking a swamp. On the high ground, manageable problems lend themselves to solution through the application of research-based theory and technique. In the swampy lowland, messy confusing problems defy technical solutions. The irony of this situation is that the problem of the high ground tends to be relatively unimportant to individuals or society at large, however great their technical interest may be; while in the swamp lie the problems of greatest human concern. (1987, p.3)

Contemporary research focus has been on the 'high ground' rather than the 'messiness' oppressed people experience in the 'swamp.' The focus on individual behavioral change ignores the basic fact that people are quintessentially social beings. Reid brilliantly captures the consequences of narrowing our professional perspective:

> An intervention may be effective in reducing a problem of classroom behavior of a child in an inner-city school, but this kind of effective practice could be challenged on the grounds that social work resources might be better spent involving community members in changing a school that is chaotically managed and under-funded. Such a school might not only produce an unending stream of classroom behavior problems but might be making a mockery of the very idea of providing decent education for the children attending. (2002, p. 277)

The group is the natural modality, the modality of choice for people to experience the potential healing and power of collective action inherent in groups. The healing power of receiving help while simultaneously helping others, of extending oneself to another person, is too often ignored. The power associated with collective action is even less on the radar screen. It is certainly not reimbursable.

The presenter apologizes for preaching to the converted. He is losing some of his energy for preaching to the unconverted. He has become progressively discouraged that most of our colleagues in the academy and agency world cannot and do not want to see what we see, and know what we know. In a comprehensive review, for example, of a decade of social group work research, ,Tolman and Molidor (1994) carefully examined 54 studies. Most of these studies evaluated the effectiveness of cognitive behavioral interventions. The authors' discovery is astonishing: namely, only four out of the 54 studies 'reported systematic measurement of any aspect of group process' (p. 155). Moreover, most studies made no mention of group process at all and only several studies even 'acknowledged the importance of group process' (p. 155). Only two studies 'attempted statistical analysis to examine the impact of small group differences' (p. 155).

While this review is several years old, how valid and relevant were these type of findings when they excluded mutual aid and peer learning as part of its treatment intervention? These types of studies ignore the findings from the famous Hawthorne experiments in which the hidden and unexpected informal group culture turned out to be responsible for increased levels of worker productivity rather than the experimental treatment variables.

In reality, what people take out of being in a group might not be what researchers think they are in fact giving them (Andrews, 2000), so it is very possible when researchers are proclaiming the effectiveness of a cognitive behavioral intervention in changing a behavior, the group members may be responding to the group's culture and the support and demands from fellow members.

Research designs for evaluating effectiveness outcomes are increasingly controlling practice rather than being flexibly and creatively responsive to the realities of practice. In order to strictly control the independent or predictor variable being tested, a significant number of designs require carefully scripted protocols, curricula, and manuals. Using a medical drug-testing paradigm, a cognitive restructuring intervention, (the experimental drug), for example, is delivered and the amount and manner of information provided to the group about cognitive distortions or managing anger (the dosage) is standardized and prescribed by a protocol or manual for the purpose of maintaining the integrity of the experimental or treatment variable. In other words, practitioners apply a standardized intervention to groups and evaluate its 'effectiveness.'

In my teaching, faculty field advising staff development seminars, and consultations, I have found that students and practitioners have become more preoccupied with protocols, curricula, and manuals than with their group members' narratives and group processes. They present, for example, meeting with semi-voluntary adolescent groups whose members are sitting with their arms folded sending strong signals of frustration, anger and resistance. The group leaders worried about manuals and meeting 'dosage' requirements simply ignore the deafening silent 'noise.' They present, for another example, their difficulties in dealing with the testing of members in anger management groups. They focus on the prescribed curriculum and try to ignore the testing. Of course, ignoring testing, only leads to its escalation. In the classroom and workshop, when the participants role-play a testing incident, the lack of congruence is startling between how the social workers teach members to deal with anger and how they themselves deal with the anger in front of them. While they are following their manuals and protocols about how to appropriately express anger, they themselves indirectly and inappropriately, express their own frustration and anger. Essentially, while they teach the correct way to deal with and express anger, they, themselves, model how not to manage and express anger; and as we have learned in most incongruent communications, much more is 'caught' than 'taught;' people pick up what we do much more than what we say should be done.

What happened in a study conducted by Castonguay and others (1996) is very similar to my classroom, seminar and consultation experiences. When workers developed interpersonal tensions with their clients (ranging from mild dissatisfaction to overt hostility), they ignored the tensions and their sources. Instead, they increased their adherence to scripted practice. When the interpersonal strains could no longer be ignored and were finally addressed, they were identified as manifestations of the client's distorted thoughts and dysfunctional beliefs. These researchers discovered that these scripted interventions only increased the clients' resistance to counseling. Henry, Strupp, et al. (1993) (cited in Duncan, 2001) studied the work of therapists before and after they were trained in using manuals. They found that those who followed the manual tended to be more authoritarian and less supportive of their clients. They poignantly cautioned that manualized practitioners might develop better relationships with their treatment manuals than with their clients. The 'manualization' of practice has the danger of bureaucratizing and de-professionalizing group work practice and reducing professionals to being technicians rather than disciplined improvisational and artistic professionals (Duncan, 2001).

An educational group for 'at risk' 17-24-year old gay males was led by a social work intern. The group members were sexually active, and were at high risk of HIV infection. They practiced unsafe sex with their friends as well as anonymous partners. In response to these 'at risk' behaviors, the agency formulated an educational group through which information about safe sex and harm-reduction behaviors would be emphasized. A curriculum was prescribed that would teach members to reduce their self-defeating behaviors. Members were open in the first session about their high-risk behaviors. While members agreed to try the group, they did not seem invested in changing their high-risk sexual behaviors. By the third session, they began to lose interest in the intern's didactic presentations and began to withdraw from the group. The prescribed curriculum structure interfered with group members' desire to discuss their concerns and inhibited their ability to reach out to each other. When the intern presented his difficulty with this group in my class, I encouraged him to pay greater attention to the group members' underlying pain and the group's potential for mutual aid (Gitterman, 2004; Gitterman & Shulman, 2005; Shulman, 2009; Steinberg, 2004). The intern showed great courage and shifted away from the prescribed curriculum and didactic presentations. The presenter helped him to integrate the prescribed curriculum content with members' own expressions and concerns; the group's mutual aid processes instantly became a powerful healing force. The intern, to his credit, makes the courageous decision to risk setting aside the 'security blanket' of the prescribed curriculum, and to become emotionally involved with the group members (Gitterman & Germain, 2008, pp. 227-230). The presenter is pleased that some of our own members are assuming leadership in the integration of content and process (Galinsky, Terzian, & Fraser, 2006; Letendre, 2007; Letendre & Wayne, 2008; Macgowan, 2003; Macgowan & Levenson, 2003).

Jack stated, 'I had a really rough day yesterday. I told my parents that I was not going back to school next semester and that I am going to take the semester off and they became really upset. They think I am lost or something. My mother was crying and she never cries. It really upset them. I didn't expect it. They've been worried about me. They think my life is going nowhere. They told me that I am not the son they wanted me to be and that I had disappointed them.'

I emphatically shook my head from side to side.

Jack went on, 'I know they think I am not going to finish school because I am gay. Ever since I came out to them three years ago, they think my life has gone down hill. They think I have all of these negative influences in my life and that the negative influence made me decide not to return to school. I'm so pissed off at them, but it's hard because they have done so much for me.'

The room was silent. John, Mike and Steve exchanged glances indicated that they understood. I said, 'I see you guys nodding your heads. You know exactly what Jack is talking about?' Steve nodded yes and said, 'I feel the same way.' He looked at Jack and said, 'I identify with you totally. I am so angry with my parents, but it is hard for me to be mad at them because they are doing so much for me, you know what I mean. I can't help it though. Whenever I am at home there is all this tension and I know I am the cause of it. You know what I mean?'

I asked, 'What do you think the tension is about, Steve?' He answered, 'I don't know, I mean, I guess I am tense because they don't really accept me. Like sometimes when we are all at home and watching some TV, a show comes on and there is the token gay character. You know what I mean?' We all laughed knowingly. Steve continued, 'Well, I always try to bring it up and talk about it. But they won't discuss it. I really try to talk about it, but they just won't. It's crazy. It's as if a wall comes down (Steve placed his hands out as he was making a wall). Sometimes, I push a little, but then they get really tense; so I stop. It makes me mad. I mean as far as the gay thing. Like, OK, so I am gay, but it's not like it's the end of the world. You know what I mean?' 'Yes, it really hurts not to have your parents accept who you are,' I replied.

Steve continued, 'After I graduate, I am going to move into the city and be on my own and I won't have to deal with them.' Mike replied, 'My parents are great, they really are, but I am mad at them too. I treat them like shit. They have always been there for me, even when my lover died, and everything. I don't know why, but I am just a total bitch to them.'

I asked Mike, 'Any hunches what makes you so mad at them?' 'I don't know,' he said. 'I really don't. I can't help it. Do you know?'

With that question all the members looked at me. I said, 'I am not sure, but on the one hand you are appreciative of the help your parents give you, but, on the other hand, you all feel different levels of acceptance about who you are, ranging from mild disappointment to total rejection.'

John agreed, 'My parents pay for my apartment, my tuition, my living expenses, but I am not allowed to talk about being gay. It's a non secret, secret!' 'Yeah,' Jack added, 'In order to afford school, I had to live with my parents and they are financially generous with me, but not in their acceptance of who I am – I always see the disappointment and hurt in their eyes.' After a silence, I added, 'You know most guys your age go through a rough time separating from their parents, but being gay makes it much tougher, much more confusing. We grow up having our parents love us and then they find out we are gay and we become someone else. We are no longer the child they used to play with, protect, embrace. Their son is gay and for some, at least initially, they experience it as a terrible loss- a loss of their hopes and dreams. And we discover that some of their love is conditional. And then we too feel a powerful loss. What is like for you when your parents' make you feel that you are not the son they had hoped for?' Mike said, 'It's awful – the pain shoots throughout my body.' He looked down at the floor. John said with tears welling in his eyes, 'Terrible doesn't describe it – especially with my Mom. We used to be so close before I told her, and now she treats me as if I don't exist.'

A painful silence followed. Steve and Jack began to cry. Steve looked at me and said, 'It really hurts, you know what I mean?' I said, 'I do know Steve, I know what you mean and I know how it feels.' John said, 'I miss my Mom so much. She used to play with me and love me. It's really strange. She always had gay friends, but when it came to me, she couldn't accept it. Things have never been the same.' John continued to wipe away his tears and asked me, 'Does it ever get better?' I said, 'Yes, it does get better – we all find ways to heal. But what I worry most about is that you guys are acting out your pain in very self destructive ways – like punishing yourself through unsafe sex – like my parents don't care about me, so why should I care about myself.'

Steve responded, 'You know right now I feel better than I have in a long time, I really do.' John and Jack replied, 'Me too! I am not alone with this pain.' Mike agreed, 'I feel much clearer – I didn't hear any of your lectures on safe sex. Today I heard you that you cared about me – about us....'

Group members become involved with each other, sharing their grief and making deep emotional connections. The intern helps members take greater control over 'their' group, and, more importantly, greater control over their lives. In reality, however, mutual aid doesn't come easy. It has to be worked at and earned. Working with groups requires advanced skills and a profound commitment to engage group processes. For example, a social worker formed a group of pregnant adolescents. The group's purpose was for members to help one another with the effects of pregnancy on their relationships with boyfriends, parents, relatives, friends, and institutions. The group members resisted dealing with their pregnancy. We join the group as the girls were engaged in dyadic conversations (Gitterman & Germain, 2008, pp. 364-365):

Sally began talking about her boyfriend at great length. I allowed her to continue for a while and then said, 'Have any of you had similar difficulties with your boyfriends?' Sally stopped for a second, but proceeded with her story. I waited for a minute again, unsure of how to deal with the other members' lack of involvement, and asked Linda, 'Did your boyfriend react the same way as Sally's?' Linda sighed and said nothing. I waited for her to respond, but immediately Karen started saying, 'My boyfriend is wonderful, he started out as a creepo, but I blew him away.' She then told the group all the fun things they had done together.

I returned to Linda, and asked, 'What are you thinking?' Linda began to say; 'Well he doesn't even call me anymore.' Sally, Susan, and Karen started a private conversation about their male conquests. (At this moment I over-identified with Linda instead of reaching underneath the bravado for the common fear.) I turned my attention to the trio and stated firmly, possibly harshly, 'Let's give Linda a chance, and then you'll have your chance to share your experiences. It's only fair to give everybody a chance to talk.' Sally ignored me, saying, 'Oh, but listen to this' and continued with her up-beat story.

I put myself in their shoes and realized they were attempting to evade and avoid their pain. I commented, 'I know talking about some of the difficulties related to being pregnant can really be uncomfortable and hard to talk about.' Sally broke in, 'I know, but listen to this' and continued her recital of partying, staying up all night, etc. After a couple of minutes (in which I was thinking how to deal with the collective avoidance), I said, 'I really feel bad. You girls have so much pain and you could help each other so much with things going on in your life, but you are choosing to act as if you aren't pregnant, as if life is wonderful, when you and I know it ain't no fun.'

Karen began to relate how her mother hassles her; Sally and Susan immediately began to talk and to laugh. I was moved by the intensity of their resistance, their fear of dealing with such an overwhelming and powerful reality and said, 'I am sure you have noticed that every time one of you begins to talk about being pregnant and its consequences, you find something else more cheerful to talk about.'

Silence.

'I know you are feeling badly inside, can you try to share what is happened since you and others found out that you were pregnant?' Linda started to cry. Susan said, 'It's ok, Linda, I cry a lot. My father thinks I am a slut (tears came to her eyes).' Sally added, 'It's no big deal, yeah, I cry too.' I broke in and said, 'Sally, what's happening to you right now?' Sally blurted out with rage in her voice, 'OK, you wanna know, I'll tell you — my mother kicked me out of the apartment, she wants nothing to do with me.' As I put my arm around her, she began to cry, sobbing hysterically.

I doubt any curriculum could have produced this type of soulful practice. The worker has to deal with the intensity of group members' resistance and fear of dealing with such an overwhelming and powerful reality of being pregnant. Avoiding painful material and escaping into wishful thinking is an understandable coping effort. For the group to progress, however, the worker has to identify and explore dysfunctional patterns by sensitively and firmly holding members to their agreed on focus. The worker has to be prepared that challenging dysfunctional patterns may induce a momentary crisis or explosion. The intense reactions often penetrate entrenched dysfunctional processes, improving communication and relational patterns. These types of interventions are impossible to script.

In a prior symposia presentation, Salmon and Kurland (2002) cautioned that too many groups were being externally controlled by prescribed curricula content, timing, and sequencing. They explained that these groups did not have a 'suggested' curriculum; they were not curriculum 'based;' rather, they were curriculum-DRIVEN groups. These groups are driven by external prescriptions and controls. A consequence, possibly unintended, is that neither group members nor social workers have ownership of the group. Let me repeat: Neither the group members nor the social workers have ownership of the group. The funding sources own these groups. How sad! How sad!

I believe it is time for us to get mad. It is time for us to fight back. It is time for us to make AASWG a priority in or professional lives rather than an *added-on* responsibility, for if we do not fully commit ourselves to group work's survival, who will? If we are not prepared to fight for our beliefs about group work, we will witness the modality we love become increasingly used as an agent of social control.

References

Andrews, H. B. (2000). The myth of the scientist-practitioner: A reply to R. King (1998) and N. King and Ollendick (1998). *Australian Psychologist.* 35(1), 60-63.

Castonguay, L. R., Goldfried, M. R., Wiser, S., Raue, P. J., & Hayes, A. M. (1996). Predicting the effect of cognitive therapy for depression: A study of unique and common factors. *Journal of Consulting and Clinical Psychology.* 64(3), 497-504.

Coyle, G.L. (1947). *Group Experience and Democratic Values.* NY: The Women's Press.

Coyle, G.L. (1948). *Group Work with American Youth.* NY: Harper & Brothers.

Duncan, B. (2001). The future of psychotherapy; beware of the siren call of integrated care. *Psychotherapy Networker,* 25(4), 24-33, 52-53.

Galinsky M.; Terzian M.; & Fraser, M. (2006). The art of group work practice with manualized curricula. *Social Work with Groups,* 29(1), 11-26.

Gitterman, A. (2004). The mutual aid model. In C. Garvin, L. Gutierrez, & M. Galinsky (Eds.). *Handbook of Social Work with Groups* (pp. 93-110). NY: Guilford Publications.

Gitterman, A. & Germain, C. B. (2008). *The Life Model of Social Work Practice: Advances in Theory and Practice* (3rd ed.). NY: Columbia University Press.

Gitterman, A. & Shulman, L. (eds.). (2005). *Mutual Aid Groups, Vulnerable and Resilient Populations, and the Life Cycle* (3rd ed.). NY: Columbia University Press.

Henry, W. P., Strupp, H., Butler, S F., Schacht, T. E., & Binder, J. L. (1993). Effects of training in time-limited dynamic psychotherapy: Changes in therapist behavior. *Consulting and Clinical Psychology,* 61, 434-330.

Klein, A.F. (1953). *Society - Democracy - and the Group*. NY: Women's Press.

Letendre, J. (2007). Take your time and give it more: Supports and constraints to success in curricular school based groups. *Social Work with Groups*, 30(3), 65-84.

Letendre, J. & Wayne, J. (2008). Integrating process interventions into a school-based curriculum group. *Social Work with Groups*, 31(3/4), 289-305.

Macgowan, M.J. (2003). Increasing engagement in groups: A measurement based approach. *Social Work with Groups*, 26(1), 5-28.

Macgowan, M.J. & Levenson, J.S. (2003). Psychometrics of the group engagement measure with male sex offenders. *Small Group Research*, 34(2), 155-169.

Reid, W.J. (2002). Knowledge for direct practice: An analysis of trends. *Social Service Review*. 76(1), 6-33.

Schön, D.A. (1987). *Educating the Reflective Practitioner*. San Francisco, CA: Jossey-Bass Publishers.

Shulman, L. (2009). *The Skills of Helping Individual, Families, Groups and Communities* (6th ed.). NY: Brooks/Cole, Cengage Learning.

Steinberg, D.M, (2004). *The Mutual Aid Approach to Working with Groups: Helping People to Help One Another*. (2nd ed.) Binghamton, NY: Haworth Press.

Tolman, R.M. & Molidor, C.E. (1994). A decade of social group work research: Trends in methodology, theory, and program development. *Research on Social Work Practice*, 4(2), 142-159.

Wilson, G. & Ryland, G. (1949). *Social Group Work Practice*. Cambridge, MA: Houghton-Mifflin Co.

2

Orchestrating the power of a group of AASWG members in partnership for change with colleagues at a university social work program

Thelma Silver and Anna Fritz

Summary

This paper will outline the process of how one chapter of AASWG worked together in partnership with an educational institution to promote group work education including the enhancement of group work content in the curriculum. The advocacy effort by the AASWG chapter follows the group work process of change at the stages of pre-group planning, beginning, middle and ending as outlined by Toseland and Rivas (2005). The following discussion will present the evolution of the task group through these stages as it pursued enhancing social work education.

Introduction

Change is needed in group work education as the movement towards a generalist curriculum model, which began in 1969, has resulted in the decline of group work education, a phenomenon noted by Birnbaum and Wayne (2000). Moreover, while group work educational opportunities decreased, social group work practice increased. As recently reported, there has been an increase in the wide use of treatment groups and task groups in social agencies in the United States (Goodman & Munoz, 2004; Sweifach & LaPorte, 2009). This discrepancy challenges social work academic institutions and social work practitioners to better educate social work students and social workers in social group work methods.

On a national level, the Association for the Advancement of Social Work with Groups (AASWG) is an organization with the mission of support and advocacy for education and training about social work with groups (www.AASWG.org). This organization collaborates with the Council on Social Work Education (CSWE), the accrediting body for social work educational institutions, to strengthen education for practice with groups (Birnbaum & Wayne, 2000). However, while national organizations can set broad policy guidelines and educational efforts, it needs to be local communities that will put change efforts into effect in academic programs.

Pre-group planning and development

The process for promoting group work in the curriculum of local universities in one Midwest region began about 15 years ago. Over the years it has involved a few different task and advocacy groups of one local chapter of the AASWG by using macro level task groups in an evolving group process effort.

In the spring of 1996 the local chapter of the AASWG was approached by the head of the social work school of one local university to be one of 14 stakeholder groups that were giving input to them as they were reevaluating their curriculum. An Assessment Task Force

Stakeholder Group of the local chapter of the AASWG was convened as a one session group to address this request. This stakeholder group met together and provided the University with a list of skills and knowledge that should be required of social work graduates. However, the result of this process of curriculum restructuring with regard to content on group work was that it only produced an elective course on groups that few students accessed. This lack of prominence of group work in the curriculum was of great concern to the members of the local chapter of AASWG. Thus, the members of the chapter identified a need for enhanced education in group work at the University and looked for ways to address this need.

In the summer of 2003 a situation arose in which two members of the local chapter of AASWG were able to take leadership in advocating for more visibility of group work at the school, including greater content on group work in the curriculum. The two AASWG members had met the new administrator of the social work school, who invited their input for the vision of the school. This led to the two AASWG members' making a financial donation to the school to set up a lectureship program with the condition that it be used to promote group work. A second outcome was setting the agenda between the AASWG members and the social work administrator for continuing the discussion on increasing group work content in their curriculum. The two AASWG members then sought the involvement of an ad hoc sub-group of nine members of the AASWG Chapter Education Committee who were all alumni of the school.

As one reviews this pre-group planning phase, one sees some of the elements that should be considered in the formation of a group (Kurland,1978; Kurland & Salmon, 1998). These elements are need, purpose, composition, structure, content, pre-group contact, and social and agency context. There was a clarity of need and purpose of the Ad Hoc Group, namely, to engage in a cooperative effort with the educational institution to enhance group work education.

In regard to group composition (Kurland & Salmon, 1998), the members of the Ad Hoc Group were people who had similar beliefs and values about the importance of group work education; all were members of the AASWG Chapter Education Committee which had this as their agenda. The members of the Ad Hoc Group also had a similar educational background as Alumni of the university. They were also familiar with the history of the curriculum when the social work school had a richer content regarding group work.

The organizational and social context (Kurland & Salmon,1998) were also important in the formation of the Ad Hoc Group. The new administration of the school presented an opportunity for the group to impact the future direction of the school's curriculum. Moreover, the administrator was welcoming this input which created the conditions for collaboration.

Beginning phase

In the fall of 2003 the Ad Hoc Group of the Education Committee of the local chapter of the AASWG and the administration of the school of social work scheduled a meeting to pursue the agenda of enhancing social work education. The Director of the Alumni Office acted as a liaison between AASWG and the school. This also reflected the dual membership of the Ad Hoc Group as both members of the AASWG who wanted to promote group work and as Alumni who, out of concern for the school, wanted to strengthen the curriculum of the school in regards to group work. Thus, the Ad Hoc Group was part of the system that was targeted for change. This interconnection strengthened the cohesion of the group members and aided the change process. At this time it was also clear that the timing of the change was a positive factor. There was a new administration, and the institution was undergoing a curriculum review; thus, there was openness to change.

During the meeting the Ad Hoc Group and the administration acknowledged the need for increasing the visibility of group work in the curriculum. Both also agreed on how AASWG could continue to be involved in the promotion of group work at the school. The administration suggested that AASWG prepare a position statement that would outline what students need to know about groups and group work. Another objective was to promote group work at the school through an endowed lectureship on group work. Therefore, the Ad Hoc Group and the administration shared concerns and the commitment that AASWG would assist the school in their quest for change.

In the pre-group planning and beginning phases there was a clarity of tasks, namely, the promotion of group work in the school and group work content in the curriculum. This clarity of purpose and function and the establishment of goals are important in the beginning stage of a group (Kurland & Salmon, 1998; Toseland & Rivas, 2005) for a group to be effective. There was also leadership in the effort by the two Alumni who brought AASWG into the process, continued to push the agenda, and helped the Ad Hoc Group stay on task.

Moreover, the composition of the Ad Hoc Group of members who shared values about the importance of group work education and who also had a similar educational background was influential in keeping the group on task. Another important factor was that the social context and organizational context were creating the conditions of change to support the work of this group. All these factors are important in the beginning stage of groups (Kurland & Salmon, 1998) and helped create an effective advocacy group.

Middle phase

The work of the Ad Hoc Group centered on writing the position paper, which included four steps. The first step was to clearly research the historical development of group work and group work content at the school. The second step was to conduct a literature search on group work publications and document available group work literature in the school's library. The third and fourth steps were to specify the essential knowledge and essential skills of group work.

When the Ad Hoc Group met to work on these tasks, some conflict developed regarding the type of group work content that should be advocated for the curriculum. There was a disagreement about whether the content should be clinically focused, or whether it should be focused on basic foundation knowledge and skills in group work. A lively discussion occurred among the members of the Ad Hoc Group who were strongly committed to either the clinical focus or the foundation focus. After listing the possible content of each focus, members noted the common knowledge and skills of both a clinical focus and a foundation focus. This activity helped create a consensus in the group about the content. Thus, those who advocated for foundation knowledge dominated, although the position statement did state a specific need for clinical skills training in social group work practice.

By early December the Ad Hoc Group had developed a draft of the "Position Statement on Groups and Group Work". In their recommendation section, the committee presented guidelines for the knowledge and skills that they thought should be required of all social work students. They made recommendations for the expansion of content on group dynamics and small-group theory and for the expansion of content on group work in the foundation course. They also acknowledged the importance of developing clinical skills. The Ad Hoc Group presented the Position Statement to the University and the recommendations as outlined in the position statement were accepted by the school's Curriculum Committee.

The members of AASWG continued to advance the agenda of the promotion of a group work course by staying active in the process of engaging in partnering with the university. Consequently, the co-leader of the Ad Hoc Group sent a letter to the administration outlining the advocacy steps cited above that had been accomplished and asking for clarification about the status of the development of a required course in group work. The co-leader had received assurance that there were plans to develop this course for the next school year and that AASWG, Alumni, and community practitioners would be consulted during the process of course development.

During this phase there was a commonality of purpose established as the administration moved ahead with consideration of course development on a macro practice course with group content. In addition, a faculty member who was developing the course solicited the help of the Ad Hoc Group in reviewing the draft proposal of the course.

In the middle phase of the group process the Ad Hoc Group focused on some of the required activities of this work phase, namely, making decisions, solving problems, developing plans, and keeping the members informed and involved (Maier, 1963; Toseland & Rivas, 2005). Much of this work centered on the task of writing the position paper regarding group work in the curriculum.

Outcomes and ending

Through a partnership with AASWG and the school of social work, some of the major recommendations to enhance work at the school that were outlined by the Ad Hoc Group in the position statement were realized. The major goal of expansion of content in group work seemed to have been met through the development of a required course of macro methods with group work content and this course was expected to be part of the foundation curriculum. Moreover, during the development of this macro practice course the Ad Hoc Group of AASWG was consulted to review the course description and make recommendations.

In the evaluation stage of the task group, the tasks are evaluated to determine if the group's purposes have been realized (Toseland & Rivas, 2005). When the Ad Hoc Group discovered that the proposed macro practice course on macro methods had not been accepted for implementation, they needed to reevaluate the process and the ongoing tasks. It was also discovered that the new faculty members were now part of the process, and the AASWG chapter needed to decide whether or not to establish a new partnership with the new faculty in order to continue their goal to enhance group work content in the curriculum.

The decision was made to continue to advocate as the macro practice course with groups was being finalized. This meant that one of the leaders of the Ad Hoc Group continued to have contact with school faculty to inquire about the status of the course. Once this course was scheduled in the social work curriculum, the Education Committee of AASWG, several of whom were members of the Ad Hoc Group, reviewed the accomplishments of the Ad Hoc Group. It was determined that the latter group had met its goal of enhancing group work education at the school. As there was no longer a reason for the Ad Hoc Group to meet, it was disbanded.

This advocacy effort by AASWG to promote group work at the University accomplished some of the tasks established in the position paper. There was a clarity of focus outlined in the position paper that enabled the Ad Hoc Group to be clear about its direction as the members went through the advocacy process. Once the task was accomplished, the group ended.

Summary and conclusion

This paper outlines how one chapter of the AASWG utilized a task group, the Ad Hoc Group, to engage with a social work education program to expand group work education. The efforts of the Ad Hoc Group were presented as proceeding through the stages of group

-- pre-group planning, beginning, middle and ending -- as outlined by Toseland and Rivas (2005).

The discussion also utilized the planning model presented by Kurland and Salmon (1998) to identify the factors that were important in the formation, cohesion and effectiveness of the Ad Hoc Group, especially need and purpose, content, group composition and social and organizational context.

As stated above, the Ad Hoc Group had a defined purpose (Kurland & Salmon, 1998) to enhance social group work education in a specific social work program and this clear task kept the group focused on its goal. Moreover, the composition of the Ad Hoc Group included people who had a strong commitment to the task of furthering group work education since, as members of the AASWG, they were committed to group work. Furthermore, as alumni of the University, they were also concerned about the lack of attention to group work at the school and wanted to change this.

As described above, the organizational context was ripe for change (Kurland & Salmon, 1998) because of the new administration and a curriculum review. The environmental context also included AASWG involvement and the financial resources of the alumni. In addition, the use of groups in agencies had increased, which possibly also put pressure on the institution to respond. All of these factors of group planning led to an effective beginning for the Ad Hoc Group as it had clarity of purpose and function. Moreover, there was leadership by the two alumni who initiated the advocacy effort by establishing the lectureship, and beginning the collaboration with the University.

In the work phase (Toseland & Rivas, 2005), the Ad Hoc Group was able to stay focused on the task of writing the position statement on group work. Conflict in this process arose about whether there should be a foundation focus or a clinical focus; the commonality of values and beliefs about the importance of group work and the shared educational background helped the group achieve a consensus.

The group also evaluated its progress in the achievement of its goals and continued to pursue its goals of creating a required group work course until this was finalized. Then, once the task was accomplished and the goal was achieved, the Ad Hoc Group was quickly ended.

In reviewing the stages (Toseland & Rivas, 2005) of the Ad Hoc Group, one can see the effective progression through the planning, beginning, and middle stages. However, the ending stage was abrupt without an evaluation of the group process that may have been useful. Instead of the focus on process at that stage, the focus was on the accomplishment of the task. Toseland and Rivas (2005) state that this balance of process and task is often a challenge in task groups.

Enhancing social work education needs to involve both practitioners and educators. Both types of social workers were involved in this advocacy effort, since the Ad Hoc Group included both clinicians and University personnel. Moreover, the Ad Hoc Group partnered with educators from the social work school to increase group work education at the school.

This advocacy effort demonstrates the power of a group to influence change; in this example a group of social workers was able to impact on changing the education at a social work school to include more group work content. Thus, for social workers who are committed to group work, this group advocacy effort may serve as an example of a way to impact on social group work education on a local level.

To engage in this type of advocacy effort, it was important to have effective planning as a group. Moreover, group composition (Kurland & Salmon, 1998) was a part of this planning as the group had the commonality of being alumni of the targeted program. Therefore, in planning this type of advocacy effort, one needs to consider the power of alumni as a group to affect change at their alma mater.

Organization and social context are also important for change efforts (Kurland & Salmon, 1998) and in this advocacy effort the organization had an administrative change and was undergoing curriculum change. As a result, the time was ripe to impact on the organization. This indicates that the group needs to evaluate the context to determine the possibility of change. At the present time, schools of social work are undergoing change as they reorganize to meet the new standards for CSWE. This may be an opportune time to impact on local institutions to enhance group work education.

It has been documented that there has been a decrease in social group work education, while the need for group work has increased (Sweifach & LaPorte, 2009). Social workers committed to group work need to recognize that they can impact this situation. This article demonstrates how one group of social workers had an impact on enhancing group work education. This can serve as an example for others to advocate change at the local universities.

References

Birnbaum, M.L., & Wayne, J. (2000). Groupwork in foundation generalist education: The necessity for curriculum change. *Journal of Social Work Education*, 36(2), 347-356.

Goodman, H. & Munoz, M. (2004). Developing social group work skills for contemporary agency practice. *Social Work with Groups*, 27(1), 17-33.

Gummer, B. (1987). Groups as substance and symbol: Group processes and organizational politics. *Social Work with Groups*, 10 (2), 25-39.

Kirst-Ashman, K. K., & Hull, G. H., Jr. (1997). *Generalist Practice with Organizations and Communities*. Chicago: Nelson-Hall.

Kurland, R. (1978). Planning: The neglected component of group development. *Social Work with Groups*, 1 (2), 173-178.

Kurland, R. & Salmon, R. (1998). *Teaching a Methods Course in Social Work with Groups*. Alexandria, VA: Council on Social Work Education.

Kurland, R, Salmon, R., Bitel, M., Goodwin, H., Ludwig, K., Wolfe Newmann, E., & Sullivan, N. (2004). The survival of social group work: A call to action. *Social Work with Groups*, 27(1), 3-17.

Maier, N. (1963). *Problem-Solving Discussions and Conferences: Leadership methods and skills*. New York: McGraw-Hill.

Sweifach, J. & LaPorte, H. H., (2009). Group work in foundation generalist classes: Perceptions of students about the nature and quality of their experience. *Social Work with Groups*, 32(4), 303-314.

Toseland, R. W. & Rivas, R. F. (2005). *An Introduction to Group Work Practice*. (5th ed.) Boston, MA: Pearson.

3
Mentoring in groups

Cheryl D. Lee and Eliette del Carmen Montiel

Introduction

This paper defines and discusses group mentoring. It provides background and a theoretical framework; discusses skills and the role of the group worker; notes benefits, barriers and multi-cultural components; offers a case example; and suggests recommendations for future research and practice.

Mentoring is typically described as a one-on-one relationship between a mentor, who shares experiences and provides guidance, and a mentee, who is relatively new to the chosen field of work or education (Buell, 2004; Dubois, Holloway, Valentine, & Cooper, 2002; Girves, Zepeda & Gwathmey, 2005; Scisney-Matlock & Matlock, 2001). It has been shown to be effective at increasing graduation rates, at ensuring employee success, at reducing stress, and at raising self-esteem (Cole, 2007; Girves et al., 2005; Scisney-Matlock & Matlock, 2001). However, group mentoring can be as or even more effective than individual mentoring in that it creates a source of social support and network for the mentees as well individual support (Girves et. al., 2005; Hadjioannou, Shelton, Fu, & Dhanarattigannon, 2007; Otis & Loeffler, 2005).

Definitions

Although it may begin with academic advising or role modeling, mentoring is much more than this; it is a multidimensional, dynamic, reciprocal relationship between a more advanced practitioner and a novice (Healy, 1997). Through sponsorship and recognition a mentor supports the growth and development of the mentees and bears in mind their long-term educational and professional goals. Moreover, the mentor also provides emotional or personal support through role modeling, encouraging, and advising (Davidson & Foster-Johnson, 2001; Gonzalez-Figueroa & Young, 2005).

Interactive group mentoring is an alternative to the traditional two-person mentoring relationship. Group mentoring programs place a successful organization veteran with a group of less-experienced prodigies. Members exchange ideas, analyze issues, receive feedback, and obtain guidance as a group. In the process they bond as a group (Buell, 2004), which gives opportunities for members with common situations to share experiences, ways of coping, and strategies for problem solving. It is also a means of developing a support network and community. Participants bring knowledge and experience to the group and increase their knowledge and comfort, essentially functioning as co-facilitators (Sands & Solomon, 2003). In a social work mentoring group there would be also a social action component (Breton, 2006).

Historical roots of group mentoring and review of current literature

Group mentoring reflects the tri-partite historical roots of social group work – the settlement house, the progressive education, and the recreation movements of the early 20th century (Breton, 2006; Ephross, 2005; Gitterman, 2006; Toseland & Rivas, 2005; Weiner, 1964). For example, Jane Addams and other settlement house workers were mentors to immigrants who came to the settlement houses for assistance. Similar to the immigrants who sought help with jobs, family concerns, and difficulties adjusting to mainstream society's demands, an increasing number of people seeking mentoring are from oppressed populations and/or of lower socio-economic status. They desire empowerment and success in navigating professional and educational systems. Educational and work organizations have programs that match people with professionals who guide, support and give resources to those who aspire to achieve their dreams.

The progressive educational movement recognized the power of peer groups to foster democratic participation and cooperative learning (Dewey, 1916). This movement espoused that it was not only the all-knowing teacher who provided information in a classroom but that students and especially adult learners also brought knowledge and experiences that would benefit everyone, including the teacher. Relating this theory to group mentoring, the mentor has knowledge and wisdom, but the mentee also arrives in the group with strengths, ideas, and experiences that benefit others in the group as well as the mentor/group worker.

The recreation movement emphasized that people would grow from participating together in enjoyable activities (Ephross, 2005). Not only do meaningful conversations create a cohesive and productive group, but the process of getting together for entertaining activities, such as outings, attending or presenting at conferences, or having celebrations is also enriching.

In a recent study Horace (2004) demonstrated the value of group mentoring as a way to provide guidance, support, and resources for nine adolescents who were faced with the challenge of deciding what to do with their lives after high school, attending college or entering the work force. The adolescents attended large public high schools, received average grades and were involved in an agency that provided mentoring groups and summer camp for inner city youth. Since the teens had average grades they were often overlooked by their high school guidance counselors, while information and resources about college were generally not provided. Group mentoring during the school year at the agency and during the summer at camp provided a venue for the adolescents to come together and help each other through the college planning process—choosing the right schools and majors, completing applications, getting information about financial aid, etc. The group became a place where these adolescents shared their feelings, fears, and hopes with one another and with a mentor who was a group worker. This paper supports the view that group mentoring can be efficient, especially with overlooked populations such as students who may have average grades but still desire to attend college.

Girves, Zepeda, and Gwathmey (2005) have demonstrated that alternative mentoring in collaborative groups can improve retention and success of women college students who have been encouraged to enter the historically under-represented fields of science and engineering. In that study college students were assigned mentors to assist in research and then presented the research at student networking conferences. These authors also discuss the importance of an infrastructure at the university level, which can support mentoring of students along with mentoring of junior faculty members.

A study by Hadjioannou, Shelton, Fu, and Dhanarattigannon (2007) demonstrated the value of a mentoring group of Ph.D. students and a professor. The article discusses how difficult, lonely, and stressful a Ph.D. program was for students who were older and returning to graduate school, balancing a rigorous academic program, work, and families or for international students far from home with language and cultural differences. That mentoring group created a place and opportunity for students to exchange information about the program, to share materials, to receive emotional support, to exchange ideas about college teaching, and to obtain peer reviews of their writing. The article also addresses the role of the mentor/professor and states that distinct differences exist between a doctoral seminar and group mentoring. That is, the mentor/professor assumes the role of a member in the mentoring group, not an authority figure, as he or she might in a seminar or a traditional classroom.

Theories

Life model theory, which asserts that people encounter stresses during life transitions, while experiencing hostile environments, and/or when interpersonal maladaptive processes exist (Gitterman & Shulman, 2005), applies to group mentoring. A mentoring group can provide support, understanding and resources to help members cope with these situations. The mentor and mentees have to carefully attend/tune in to understand the issues confronting members (Gitterman, 2005). Empowerment theory also has a good fit with mentoring groups, because mentees frequently emanate from oppressed groups and are seeking empowerment to navigate through mainstream systems. Freire (1993) and Breton (2006) advise that the oppressed must not only raise their consciousness regarding environmental oppression but also must change the environment to make it more hospitable. Finally, social group work theory in general and especially mutual aid theory (Gitterman, 2005; Gitterman & Shulman, 2005; Schwartz, 1972) applies to group mentoring. The group worker mediates individual, group, and agency needs and lends a vision of hope; group members need, support and hold each other accountable; a contract is negotiated; resources are shared; dialectical and authentic communication transpires among members; the *all in the same boat* phenomenon reassures; and a strengths-based perspective is paramount where members are respected, not judged, and appreciated for their strengths.

Skills and the role of the group worker

Skills utilized in group mentoring reflect social work group practice. In the beginning of the process the group worker is more active as s/he plans, gathers members into the group, and orients members regarding the purpose of the group. S/he is comfortable with authority and is more directive and structured in the first couple of sessions in order to model behaviors for the members before asking members, for example, to introduce themselves to the group. The group worker is honest with the members regarding the group's purpose, and there are no hidden agendas (Kurland & Salmon, 1999). A contract is made between the members and the group worker, and input from the members is sought. For example, if in the mentoring process it is expected that mentees discuss personal problems in order to see how these issues affect their professional success, then this purpose should be brought out in initial discussions with the group.

Ephross (2005) points out that being still and listening is a major skill of the group worker so that members can be free to talk and reflect. The worker may also initiate round-robin discussions, where each mentee takes a turn discussing something on his or her mind while the other members comment. This is a good technique for a mentoring group in order to make sure that no one feels excluded or dominates the session. The worker may comment about similar and different themes expressed by members in order to nurture cohesiveness or model acceptance of difference. The group worker also summarizes and reaches for members' input in order to illustrate where the group has been and where it might go, while checking in and clarifying issues during process are other helpful techniques (Ephross, 2005; Toseland & Rivas, 2005). The worker may initiate exercises and/or activities in order to maintain members' interest, such as role playing, which is useful to help members practice interactions that apply outside of the group. Finally, if confronting is employed during any part of group process, it should be combined with support and intended as a way of helping a member or the whole group to progress (Steinberg, 2006).

The group worker in this type of group shares information that may not be available to the members due to their lack of status and experience with the host setting. The group worker may offer information about different positions/promotions that are available and how members can make themselves marketable for these positions. Group members often also have ideas to share with other members.

Commitment on the part of the group worker is paramount to the success of the group (Ephross, 2005). S/he must show deep interest in the members, and s/he must structure regular contact. In addition, the group worker must keep abreast of the group work literature in order to foster creativity and scientifically-based knowledge, to provide a safe environment in a changing multi-cultural world, and to inspire ethical behavior.

Benefits and barriers

The literature has shown that mentoring helps students and employees to progress in their chosen paths. Students involved in mentoring experiences with faculty members have demonstrated greater academic success (Cole, 2007; Girves, Zepeda, & Gwathmey, 2005; Scisney-Matlock & Matlock, 2001). This is especially true for minority and otherwise oppressed people who may not have role models with higher education or professional positions in the work force (Cole, 2007; Dubois, Holloway, Valentine, & Cooper, 2002;

Girves et. al., 2005; Scisney-Matlock & Matlock, 2001). Individual mentoring does not reach many people who could benefit, and thus group mentoring is potentially more efficient in reaching larger numbers. There is also a ripple effect of group mentoring where mentees go on to mentor others (Girves, Zepeda, & Gwathmey, 2005). The mentor also grows in this process and self esteem rises especially when mentees succeed (Atkins & Williams, 1995). Members of a group benefit from the multiple sources of mutual aid present in a group not found in individual mentoring. There is an opportunity to build long-lasting friendships and a community, both of which endure after the termination of the mentoring group (Girves, Zepeda, & Gwathmey, 2005).

The barriers to group mentoring are that first, it is a relatively new concept and thus may not be embraced by an agency, institution or individuals. Second, there is a dearth of literature and research about this phenomenon. Also, individuals may not want to share time with a mentor. The logistics of gathering people with busy schedules and diverse locations for a meeting may also present obstacles. Confidentiality may be worrisome; and finally, some cultures may not support sharing, such as revealing private family matters or problems to a group of peers or even to a professional (Fluhr, 2004).

Cultural considerations

Diversity issues must be considered in mentoring. Twenty-nine percent of entering college students comes from minority ethnic groups, and it is expected that enrollment will be at about 40% in the next two decades (Cole, 2007). Further, many non-minority workers are retiring, and it is estimated that by 2028 40% of jobs in the U.S. will need to be filled by members of minority groups with advanced technical skills (Girves, Zepeda, & Gwathmey, 2005). Colleges and universities include many minority students who want their mentors to respect their differences and cultural values (Scisney-Matlock & Matlock, 2001). They are naturally sensitive and will distance themselves if mentors appear to have biases or project stereotypes onto them. However, mentees also may have difficulty adjusting to a school or work situation because of cultural variables and will want to be able to freely discuss these issues with a mentor (Scisney-Matlock & Matlock, 2001). According to Scisney-Matlock & Matlock (2001), every professor should be willing to mentor students; the burden should not be placed on professors of color to mentor all students of color.

There are, however, mixed results in the research regarding matching race/ethnicity and gender in mentoring relationships. A meta-analysis of 55 studies found that ethnicity or gender of the mentor does not appear to influence academic success (Dubois, Holloway, Valentine, & Cooper, 2002); rather, it is the quality of the mentoring relationship that has bearing on student success. Kurland (2002) supports this finding in her narrative about cross-cultural group work mentoring. A recent study (Gonzalez-Figueroa & Young, 2005) of 305 employees, however, found that ethnicity seems to be the most salient factor in success – even more important than matched gender. Girves, Zepeda, and Gwathmey (2005) recommend that different mentors should be selected for different aspects of life. For example, one mentor may assist personal life decisions while another guides academic research. Fluhr (2004), who discusses the reality of heterogeneous groups, suggests that there are ways in which members from diverse ethnic cultures, genders, and abilities can benefit from a shared group mentoring experience.

Case study

In a public university setting, a group of at-risk college students met in a mentoring group for two years. A formal mentoring program, (www.csulb.edu/partners), has been in operation for 20 years at this university in order to promote graduation rates of first generation and under-represented minority college students. These students do not have family role models who have graduated from college.

Most of the mentors/professors conduct one-on-one mentoring sessions with students. The mentor/author (Lee) discussed meeting in a group with six mentees who were transfer students who she had recruited in an entry level social work class and one freshman (an aspiring graphic arts major) assigned by the program administrator. They were advised that the purpose of the group was to help them succeed at the university and to graduate.

This was both a homogenous (mostly social work majors) and heterogeneous group (a variety of ethnic cultures, single and married students, parents and non-parents, a person with physical disabilities, etc.). The structure was closed, but two new members joined the group after the group was underway, bringing the total to nine members plus the mentor/group worker.

The group members contributed ideas to the contract. Several of the mentees wanted help in applying for graduate schools. Most wanted social support for staying in college. A few wanted involvement with a faculty member and a campus organization. Others sought assistance in mastering environmental obstacles, such as family or cultural expectations, that were interfering with their academic goals.

The group met every two weeks for an hour. The students attended night classes; therefore, meetings were scheduled before classes to promote good attendance. The group planning included recreational events, organized both by the worker and members. The mentor also convened back yard barbecues for members to energize and catch up with one another. Group members brought family members to the events, which promoted group cohesion and understanding of cultural norms; as the group trust level increased over time, sensitive and/or taboo topics began to surface.

In the middle stage of this group, work was related to passing courses, to being successful at field internships, and to applying for graduate schools. The middle stage was not confined to academic support, however, but also dealt with personal issues that affected their education, such as family life or work. The mentor promoted full participation so that no one was excluded, and as common themes were highlighted, members lent one another their support, and ultimately developed a supportive *all in the same boat* feeling.

Over time the mentoring group became quite cohesive. As one of the mentees who joined the group at the beginning of its second year exclaimed, *No one in classes is friendly toward me, but I finally feel I've made good friends with the social work students in here.* In many sessions members discussed differences and similarities in their cultures and how their cultures either provided support, such as spiritual guidance, or barriers, such as expectations of marriage before they felt ready. When all members discussed their financial struggles, the mentor was able to identify scholarship opportunities.

In the second year there was also a social action component to the group. The mentor asked if members wanted to present the group's work to an annual international symposium sponsored by the Association for the Advancement of Social Work with Groups (AASWG). Mentees agreed enthusiastically, and the group became a task group with a goal of writing a proposal, creating the presentation, practicing, and evaluating. The students marveled at what they had accomplished by presenting, volunteering, and networking at an international social group work conference and felt empowered; while the audience was impressed about the support for this mentoring program from the university. As one mentee stated, *We could show that we were not just measly students.*

In the termination stage group members evaluated the accomplishments over the two-year period and even met without the mentor to plan a terminating surprise. All members reported that they found the group mentoring to be valuable for their academic success, and in spite of incredible obstacles, which included caring for children and older adults, financial hardships, and illness, all of the students graduated. They also obtained jobs in human services, and several made plans to attend graduate school.

Summary and recommendations for research and practice

This paper has defined and discussed group mentoring, has offered a brief history and literature review, has discussed skills and the role of the mentoring-group worker, has identified benefits and obstacles, has highlighted some cultural considerations, and has provided a case study of a group-mentoring experience. As we enter an era of baby boomer retirement, group mentoring stands out as a promising and efficient method of insuring a productive and humane work force, and it has been suggested by some that baby boomer retirees should actively serve as group work mentors (Dubois, Holloway, Valentine, & Cooper, 2002). However, mentoring groups need to be documented, studied, and both their process and outcomes evaluated so that this method of helping people can meet its full potential.

Social service agencies and educational institutions should establish formal mentoring programs, given that much of the literature indicates that formal mentoring programs have better outcomes due to the structure, monitoring, and support of the host agency (Dubois et al., 2002; Girves, Zepeda, & Gwathmey, 2005). Further, systems should consider group mentoring as opposed to individual mentoring in order to serve more people without sacrificing quality, as group process has the advantage of mutual aid. Finally, mentors need to be supported by the host system, as mentoring is stimulating work but also takes time and energy to do well. In sum, group work has demonstrated that it can make life happier and less stressful for people who participate in groups, and group mentoring appears to be no exception.

References

Atkins, S. & Williams, A. (1995). Registered nurses' experiences of mentoring undergraduate nursing students. *Journal of Advanced Nursing*, 21: 1006-1015.

Breton, M. (2006). An empowerment perspective. In C. Garvin, L. Gutiérrez, & M. Galinsky, (Eds.), *Handbook of Social Work with Groups* (pp. 58-75). New York: The Guilford Press.

Buell, C. (2004). Models of mentoring in communication. *Communication Education*, 53(1), 56-73.

Cole, D. (2007). Do interracial interactions matter? An examination of student-faculty contact and intellectual self-concept. *The Journal of Higher Education*, 78(3), 249-281.

Davidson, M.N., & Foster-Johnson, L. (2001). Mentoring in the preparation of graduate researchers of color. *Review of Educational Research*, 71, 549-574.

Dewey, J. (1916). *Democracy and Education.* NY: Macmillan

Dubois, D.L., Holloway, B., Valentine, J.C., & Cooper, H. (2002). Effectiveness of mentoring programs for youth: A meta-analytic review. *American Journal of Community Psychology*, 30(2), 157-197.

Ephross, P.H. (2005). Social work with groups: Practice principles. In G. Grief & P. H. Ephross (Eds.), *Group Work with Populations at Risk* (pp. 1-12). New York: Oxford University Press.

Fluhr, T. (2004). Transcending differences: Using concrete subject-matter in heterogeneous groups. *Social Work with Groups*, 27 (2/3), 35-54.

Freire, P. (1993). *Pedagogy of the Oppressed.* NY: Continuum. (Original work published 1970)

Girves, J.E., Zepeda, Y., & Gwathmey, J.K. (2005) Mentoring in a post-affirmative action world. *Journal of Social Issues,* 61 (3), 449-479.

Gitterman, A. (2005). Building mutual support in groups. *Social Work with Groups,* 12(2), 91-106.

Gitterman, A. (2006). The mutual aid model. In D. Garvin, L. Gutiérrez, & M. Galinsky (Eds.), *Handbook of Social Work with Groups, 2nd ed.* (pp. 93-110) New York: The Guilford Press.

Gitterman, A., & Shulman, L. (2005) The life model, oppression, vulnerability, resilience, mutual aid, and the mediating function. In A. Gitterman & L. Shulman (Eds.), *Mutual Aid Groups, Vulnerable and Resilient Populations, and the Life Cycle, 3rd ed.* (pp. 3-37). New York: Columbia University Press.

Gonzalez-Figueroa, E., & Young, A.M. (2005). Ethnic identity and mentoring among Latinas in professional roles. *Cultural Diversity and Ethnic Minority Psychology,* 11(3), 213-226.

Hadjioannou, X., Shelton, N.R., Fu, D., & Dhanarattigannon, J. (2007). The road to a doctoral degree: Co-travelers through a perilous passage. *College Student Journal,* 41(1), 160-177.

Healy, C.C. (1997). An operational definition of mentoring. In H.T. Frierson, Jr. (Ed.), *Diversity in Higher Education: Mentoring and Diversity in Higher Education* (Vol. I, pp. 9-22). Greenwhich, Connecticut: JAI Press.

Horace, C. (2004). One group's journey from camp to college. *Social Work with Groups,* 27(4), 31-50.

Kurland, R. (2002). Racial difference and human commonality: The worker-client relationship. *Social Work with Groups,* 25(1/2), 113-118.

Kurland, R., & Salmon, R. (1998). Purpose: A misunderstood and misused keystone of group work practice. *Social Work with Groups,* 21(3), 5-17.

Kurland, R., & Salmon, R. (1999). *Teaching a Methods Course in Social Work with Groups.* Alexandria, VA: CSWE.

Otis, M.D., & Loeffler, D.N., (2005). Changing youths' attitudes toward difference: A community-based model that works. *Social Work with Groups,* 28(1), 41-64.

Sands, R.G., & Solomon, P. (2003). Developing educational groups in social work practice. *Social Work with Groups,* 26(2), 5-21.

Schwartz, W. (1986). The group work tradition and social work practice. In A. Gitterman & L. Shulman (Eds.), *The Legacy of William Schwartz: Group Practice as Shared Interaction* (pp. 7-27). New York: Haworth Press.

Scisney-Matlock, M. & Matlock, J. (2001). Promoting understanding of diversity through mentoring undergraduate students. *New Directions for Teaching and Learning*, 2001, 75-84.

Steinberg, D.M. (2006). The art, science, heart and ethics of social group work: Lessons from a great teacher. In A. Malekoff, R. Salmon, & D. M. Steinberg (Eds.), *Making Joyful Noise: The Art, Science and Soul of Group Work*, pp. 33-45.

Toseland, R. & Rivas, R.F. (2005). *An Introduction to Group Work Practice* (5th ed.). Boston: Allyn & Bacon.

Weiner, H.J. (1964). Social change and social group work practice. *Social Work*, 9: 106-112.

4

A magical mystery tour:
Education and social work with groups across borders

Ellen Sue Mesbur

Summary

This paper describes the use of social group work in teaching in Russia across language, culture, history and tradition. A qualitative analysis of small group tasks and discussions will demonstrate the universal themes of social work practice and education. Examples of the classes 'in action' will illustrate the engagement of participants in what was for them, and for the instructor, a unique learning experience.

Introduction

This paper describes my experience of the use of social group work in teaching in Russia across language, culture, history and tradition. I was invited to participate in the development and delivery of a Field Education Training Program in Russia as part of an international project, the Canada–Russia Disability Program (CRDP). The multi-year, multi-million dollar project, funded by the Canadian International Development Agency, included Canadian representatives of social work education, government, non-government and disability communities. The project was undertaken using a tripartite model of engagement including the voluntary, government and education sectors in both Canada and Russia. Activities were focused within four components: education, demonstration models, policy promotion, and network and information dissemination in three Russian cities: Moscow, Stavropol, and Omsk. The project encompassed three streams: Social Work, Mental Health, and Disability Studies.

I will begin by laying out the social and historical context and the state of social work practice and education in Russia. Further, the tensions around cross-national teaching in social work in the context of international development assistance will be discussed. The following brief section of the paper will describe the teaching context and the characteristics of the participants. I will continue by outlining the conceptual framework for the social group work approach utilized for the training and illustrate the use of this method with examples from the training. Next, the qualitative analysis of major themes generated by the participants through classroom discussions will be presented. I will conclude with my reflections on this unique learning experience.

Leviathan: Social change and the rise of social work in Russia

For more than two decades after the collapse of the Soviet Union, Russia has been going through a 'transition,' a complex social transformation that includes the replacement of the communist state and planned economy with a capitalist free-market and democratic institutions. Such rapid political, social, and economic change has rendered Russia akin to a third world country – experiencing widespread and endemic social problems such as unemployment, poverty, and homelessness without the necessary social infrastructure and supports to address or ameliorate them (Freed, 1995; Templeman, 2001). The resultant social, economic, and political conditions have revealed acute social welfare needs requiring the development and expansion of a social service infrastructure and a workforce of professionally educated and trained social workers (George, 1999; Gray & Simpson, 1998; Tunney, 2001; Whitmore & Wilson, 1997).

As a result, in the early 1990's, the first formal social work training programs were introduced in Russia, alongside a fledgling targeted social welfare system, replacing the Soviet-type universal social assistance and protection (Kolkov, Shapiro & Solovyov, 2000; Rutgers University Center, 2008; Templeman, 2001). The decade following perestroika saw the emergence of three professional social work associations, specialized periodicals, and over 150 schools of social work in Russia (Iarskaia-Smirnova, Romanov & Lovtsova, 2004; Penn, 2007; Templeman, 2001). Despite these promising initial steps, social work as a profession in Russia remains in its early phase of formation and faces many challenges as well as pedagogical obstacles (Iarskaia-Smirnova & Romanov, 2008; Iarskaia-Smirnova, Romanov & Lovtsova, 2004; Penn, 2007).

For example, the majority of those working in the social services industry in Russia have no formal training or education (Iarskaia-Smirnova & Romanov, 2002; Templeman, 2001). Yet, in spite of this it is commonplace for those working in social services to self identify as social workers and to be recognized as such (Templeman, 2001). Additionally, social work credentials have yet to be established, and informal professional standards and a code of ethics are known by only a small group of Russian educators and graduates (Iarskaia-Smirnova & Romanov, 2002). Moreover, social workers are typically viewed as welfare workers or, as they are commonly referred to, 'visitors,' and are charged with such commonplace tasks as aiding clients with their house chores and purchasing groceries rather than providing professional interventions (Kolkov, Shapiro & Solovyov, 2000; Iarskaia-Smirnova & Romanov, 2002; Templeman, 2001). The profession's lack of legitimacy is reinforced by the limited funding of social services and low salaries of social workers, who are predominantly women (Iarskaia-Smirnova & Romanov, 2008).

Similarly to professional practice, social work education in Russia faces major challenges. First, with such a brief history, social work theory relevant to the post-Soviet context is underdeveloped, while social work theories and approaches traditionally grounding social work in Western countries face cultural barriers in Russia (Penn, 2007). Second, an understanding of the scope of practice is limited. Few guidelines exist for social workers, and many workers are untrained, having entered the profession as a result of governmental, economic, and social changes (Templeman, 2001). Likewise, most social work instructors do not have social work education (Penn, 2007). Next, social work training in Russia has been criticized for the weak integration between theoretical education and practice (Penn, 2007; Rutgers University Center, 2008). Furthermore, field education suffers from the lack of regulation of the relationship between universities and social work agencies and from the lack of supervision of students' fieldwork (Penn, 2007). Overall, social work training is geared toward general education, and programs of study in specialized areas of practice and/ or with specific populations are insufficient (Rutgers University Center, 2008). Unsurprisingly, the attrition of social work students is high (Penn, 2007); moreover, less than 30% of social work graduates become employed in the profession (Iarskaia-Smirnova & Romanov, 2002).

International technical assistance: Can social work knowledge be transferred across borders?

Since social work started to emerge and grow in post-Soviet countries, the need for technical assistance to strengthen professional practice and education was recognized both by foreign aid agencies and local counterparts (Rutgers University Center, 2008; Trygged & Eriksson, 2009). A number of internationally-funded projects and programs to support various areas of social work in Russia have been reported in the literature (Rutgers University Center, 2008). Also, Western universities have been involved in building the capacity of social work educators in Russia and in a variety of activities, including providing access to information, sharing educational materials, expert assistance with curriculum development, scholar exchange, and faculty training (Penn, 2007; Rutgers University Center, 2008).

While there has been genuine and mutual desire to share knowledge on the part of Western social workers and to adopt knowledge on the part of Russian counterparts, the outcomes of these activities have been mixed in introducing and sustaining new approaches to practice and training. For instance, Trygged and Erikkson (2009) describe the difference in the outcomes of two similar projects aimed at transferring Swedish social work models to Russia. Likewise, Penn (2007) reports obstacles to international collaboration in social work from the perspective of Russian partners, who often found that foreign models are not suitable for the Russian context and need to be adjusted, felt that 'Western visitors' cannot understand the experiences of local partners and believed that local actors had limited contribution to the project decision making.

The conventional asymmetry-based approach to capacity building has been heavily criticized for being colonial in spirit and was held responsible for foreign aid that brought limited benefit to receiving countries (Torres, 2001). According to Torres (2001), the asymmetry-based aid has an inherent assumption that universal and high-quality knowledge can (only) be produced by an aid-giving party for an aid-receiving party; consequently, capacity building has been predominantly expert-driven, while the local expertise of those who work in the field is often devaluated and ignored. As a result, projects utilizing asymmetrical, top-down, one-way knowledge transfer approaches have lead to the introduction of models irrelevant to the local context and are therefore unsustainable (Torres, 2001). Knowledge in the international assistance context is not to be transferred; it has to be generated by participating and interacting organizations, social groups, and individuals. In this context, a knowledge-transfer model should be replaced by an interactive model of knowledge utilization, which holds that in order to be relevant and useful, knowledge has to be co-produced and validated by knowledge users (Denis, Lehoux, & Champagne, 2004). Moreover, learning in this context can be conceptualized as 'mutual trade,' an interactive, engaging experience that has an impact on all parties involved, including both local and Western participants (Doel & Penn, 2007).

The debate around asymmetry-based international technical assistance resonates with the social work profession's existential struggle to balance the contextual, specific, local and the universal, common, global (Gray & Fook, 2004). Social workers involved in international projects face a number of essential questions, such as: Is social work knowledge transferable from one social, historical, cultural context to another? Which elements of social work are universal and which ones are context-specific? Will social work theory and methods developed and tested in a Western country be relevant in a developing country? How social work approaches rooted in liberal societies' values will be accepted in a post-communist society? Finally, is cross-national technical assistance compatible with social work ethics which is sensitive to the relationships of power and inequality? While there is no definitive answer to any of these questions, social workers have to embrace the complex nature of this work that may simultaneously comprise the elements of technical assistance, neocolonialism, and mutual trade (Doel & Penn, 2007).

The teaching context

My teaching of the Field Education Training Program occurred in two cities: at the Russia State Social University (RSSU) in Moscow and at the Omsk State Technical University (OSTU) in Omsk. I taught for five days, six hours a day, in each city. The Field Education Training Program and Manual was developed to provide Russian schools of social work with the information necessary to offer comprehensive and globally recognized field instructor training to their agency-based field instructors. The content was designed to mix the broadest standards in social work education, such as the International Association of Schools of Social Work (IASSW) and the International Federation of Social Workers (IFSW) Global Standards for Social Work Education, the latest research findings from Canada and the United States, with more detailed Russian-specific information for field instructors and case-study examples to use as discussion points. The curriculum was designed to incorporate discussion activities and practical applications to maximize learning through the interaction of course content with the experience and knowledge of participants.

The two trainings brought together a range of representatives across sectors, reflecting the general diversity of the workforce in Russia. At the RSSU, between 25–40 individuals (with a gender breakdown of approximately 95% females and 5% males) participated in training, including a few students, professors of social pedagogy, social work and medical rehabilitation departments, social service providers, representatives of government, and disability organizations. At the OSTU, between 80–85 individuals participated in training (with a gender breakdown of approximately 85% females and 15% males) including students, professors, social service providers for children, youth, families and the aged, the disability community, and government. Most participants had little formal socialization to the profession of social work and no formal training in social work. In addition to local participants, representatives of the CRDP's Working Groups and participants from Stavropol region attended and participated in the training course offered in Omsk region.

Since language can be a major obstacle to effective communication in cross-national projects, the quality of translation is a crucial component of the training process. The Field Education Training Manual that I wrote had been translated into Russian, and copies were made available to the participants. Local bilingual interpreters assisted me in the course of training. In Moscow the two young translators, who were students in the Department of Languages, worked diligently beginning with a 'crash course' on social work terminology to acquaint them with the culture of the professional language. In Omsk, I initially worked with an experienced translator who was a professor in the Department of Languages, and for the last three days one of the CRDP Russian-speaking staff filled in until another experienced translator was located.

Social group work and teaching

In my teaching of the Field Education Training Program, I applied a social group work approach, drawing upon ample evidence in the literature that social group work skills can contribute to effective teaching (Birnbaum, 1984; Kurland & Salmon, 1998; Schwartz, 1960, 1980; Shulman, 1970; Somers, 1971). Schwartz (1960), who viewed teaching as a special case of the helping process in a group, identified five essential tasks of the teacher in the education experience. These tasks are as follows: searching out the common ground between the learner's perceptions of his own needs and the subject matter; detecting and challenging the obstacles which obscure the common ground; contributing data – ideas, facts, values, concepts, which are not available to the learner; 'lending a vision' to the learner in which the instructor is revealed as one whose hopes and aspirations are strongly invested in the interaction between the learner and the subject area; and defining the requirements and the limits of the learning situation.

Schwartz (1980) noted that the substance of communication and the circumstances under which it takes place must be understood as an integrated whole, encompassing both process and content. He viewed content and process as a 'seamless whole,' characterizing *how* we work and *what* we are working on as possessing the same focus and impetus. In describing the interactive nature of the teaching-learning transaction, Schwartz (1960) suggested that communication from the teacher/group worker will only be effective to the extent that '...the members are alive to the possibilities of the learning situation, feel a personal stake in its effects, and learn to use it in their own behalf. It thus remains for the worker to utilize what he knows and feels in such a way that it may become that valuable to others' (pp. 33-34).

This conceptualization framed my teaching in the Russian social work project, particularly in addressing the participants' current realities and balancing my own valuing of group process in learning with participants' experiences with a different approach to education. One cannot overestimate the challenges of teaching with translators; interacting with individuals who have different histories, cultures, languages, and frames of reference for practice; and engaging participants who have experienced mainly a didactic authoritarian tradition of education. To overcome these challenges, I adapted Schwartz's idea (1960, 1980) of teaching as a special case of the helping process in a group and drew upon personal experience in social work education to engage the participants in a 'Magical Mystery Tour' (The Beatles, 1967) of education to a social group work beat. The use of social group work in the classroom to engage the participants as group members in a collaborative journey of discovery was the key to building trust and connections and promoting cross-national professional dialogue.

The following three examples illustrate the use of social group work in cross-national teaching. The first example shows how social work was defined through the training. Social work is a contextual profession, described as a socially constructed phenomenon, an activity which is to a large extent defined by the economic, social and cultural conditions in which it takes place (Payne, 1991). Therefore, instead of being exposed to lecturing about what social work is in Canada or the US, the participants were asked to reflect on the current state of social work practice and education in Russia. In the process of developing their definitions of social work, the participants generated the following themes: (a) Practical work (social work as providing help to those people in the community in need); (b) Paradigm approach (social work as helping people in difficult life situations versus social work as an integration of a human being in society to create optimum conditions for self-realization); (c) Competencies (social work as professional knowledge and skills such as paperwork skills, communication skills, applying theoretical knowledge in practice, knowledge of the legislation to facilitate clients' access to benefits, quality of task performance, knowledge of client populations); (d) Social workers' roles.

The second example is the use of social group work to help the participants to identify what information from the field regarding societal trends, conditions, and social work needs are important for universities and their communities to know. The groups generated the following themes: (a) raising the legitimacy of the field and of social workers in the society through public awareness campaigns and higher social workers' salaries; (b) clarifying social workers' and clients' responsibilities; (c) the need for advocacy and legal protection of social workers. These findings indicate a major concern about the field's lack of recognition and social workers' being de-valued in the society.

The third example demonstrates the participants' exploration of the core values of the profession. Despite not having formal social work education and a lack of established professional codes of ethics, the participants showed strong commitment to what appeared to be the underlying values of social work. They spoke of the 'ideal' and the 'real,' with many striving for the ideal in challenging environments. The key themes emerged in the Omsk group discussion about social work values were as follows:

(a) humanism (human beings are the top priority of any society);
(b) social justice (people who need help should get help);
(c) ethics, norms, rules (specialists base their work on the national code);
(d) respect of human rights and freedom;
(e) individual approach (personal approach connected to humanism);
(f) social partnerships (effective social work efficient requires partnership between systems at government levels and different agencies and organization);
(g) a client-centered approach;
(h) personal qualities of social workers: humanity, empathy, altruism, tolerance, responsiveness, good communication skills, creativity, positive attitude, honesty, kindness, self-development; and
(i) professionalism (an integration of knowledge and experience).

As expected, social group work revealed that each participant as well as each group as a whole represented a specific historical, cultural, regional, and social context. However, I was struck by what appeared to be intuitive understandings of social work as a profession, even though the participants generally lacked the knowledge of theoretical foundations of social work. The core values and understanding of helping, the notions of professional practice and competencies, the need for knowledge, and their understandings of the limitations of their own social/political/economic context were evident in the participants' discussions.

The data generated by the participants reflect what Taylor (1999) describes as some basic, acceptable universals: firstly, that of social work's altruistic mission of helping others and preventing harm, a mission that is bolstered by a belief that society and its institutions, must be responsive to human needs and interests; secondly, social work's pursuit of social justice. One can claim that the fundamental humanitarian values of social work are transferable, whereas the social, cultural, economic and political conditions of individual countries define how these primary values are to be achieved.

In evaluating the course, the participants acknowledged an interactive, participatory social group work approach, which allowed for positive exchange among the participants and between the participants and the facilitator, as well as contributed to the friendly and open learning atmosphere in the classroom. The participants noted and greatly valued an opportunity for networking and for shared learning of knowledge, experiences and perspectives from their colleagues. Moreover, I found that a social group work approach to training was useful not only for generating knowledge through participant engagement but also for conveying certain tools while adapting them to local contexts. The participants appreciated the tools used and provided to them, in the form of small-group exercises, handouts and the course reference manual itself. Specifically identified as highly relevant and of value were modules covering 'how-to' of effective field supervision, understanding learning styles, addressing special challenges in field instruction, and operational principles of field education.

With respect to the content of the course, the majority of the participants reported a significantly better understanding of field education principles and practices as a result of their involvement in the course. The key topic areas identified as areas of learning included ethics, stress, and addressing student challenges. Specific reference was made relating to knowledge gained with respect to the Canadian context and its application to the current status of field education in Russia. Finally, the participants found that the course complemented already existing knowledge by developing links – most specifically, by providing a framework for understanding the importance of integration of theory-based knowledge with practical components of skill development in social work.

Conclusions and reflections

Teaching social work cross nationally is a formidable task that involves the challenges of teaching with translators; connecting with individuals who have different histories, cultures, languages, and frames of reference for practice; and engaging participants who have experienced mainly a didactic authoritarian tradition of education. The use of a social group work approach for teaching field education in the Russian project allowed me to engage the participants into an interactive, participatory mutual-learning process through which knowledge was generated, shared, reinvented, and interpreted by transforming participants' experiences rather than transferred as a ready-to-use product. Adapting Schwartz's idea (1960, 1980) of teaching as a special case of the helping process in a group and drawing upon personal experience in social work education, I engaged the participants in a 'Magical Mystery Tour' (The Beatles, 1967) of education to a social group work beat. Through social group work, the key to building trust and connections and promoting cross-national professional dialogue, the participants as group members - and I as a facilitator - embarked on a collaborative journey of discovery.

The discussion of cross-national teaching in social work contributes to a larger debate of the issues of Westernization-indigenization in social work and universal, international versus local, context-specific social work (Gray & Fook, 2004). Certainly, social workers participating in cross-national social work projects have to critically appraise their own assumptions of universality and transferability of their understandings of social work core values as well as approaches to practice and education. Moreover, social workers have to be open to exploring cultural, historical, social, geographical contexts different from their own backgrounds, which shape their social work practice and education. However, as Doel and Penn (2007) note, recognizing difference while ignoring what is common can be yet another form of discriminating and constructing 'the Other.' They argue that mutual learning in cross-national interaction 'can only happen when we break through the experience of difference and allow ourselves to understand the *commonalities*, too' (p.378).

There are numerous cultural challenges inherent in the role of a social work educator teaching abroad, including understanding the local needs and issues and promoting social work's professional identity (Tunney, 2002). Western social work education models cannot be simply transplanted to other countries. I was conscious of and guided by the cultural relativity of my North American view of field education programs. For instance, organizational change, social justice, and advocacy are accepted field practice goals in North America; in Russia, where the tradition of social change necessary for activism has been lost, creation of an organization around a profession has yet to be achieved. Notions of 'advocacy' for vulnerable persons, for example, are difficult to promote when general cultural attitudes in Russia view persons with disabilities and physical and mental illnesses as 'defective' (Tunney, 2002). This view was reinforced when participants in my classes discussed programs of 'correctology.' Yet, throughout both courses, participants noted the need for advocacy, promotion of human rights, and structural changes in society.

A qualitative analysis of data generated by the participants of the training through small-group tasks and discussions demonstrates the universal themes of social work practice and education in two Russian cities. While the social, cultural, and historical differences between North American social work and social work emerging in post-communist Russia are hard to overestimate, Russian social workers grapple with issues familiar to their colleagues across borders: issues of social work ethics, client-worker relationships, professional competencies, integration of social work theory and practice, and the place of the field in the society. My experience with the participants in Russia taught me that we have much to learn from each other. Through that journey—a 'Magical Mystery Tour'—in two Russian cities, the commonalities of a commitment to humanity and the fundamental principles of social work and social work field education were articulated and shared once again.

References

Birnbaum, M. (1984). The integration of didactic and experiential learning in the teaching of group work. *Journal of Education for Social Work,* 20(1), 50-58.

Denis, J-L., Lehoux, P., & Champagne, F. (2004). A knowledge utilization perspective in fine-tuning dissemination and contextualizing knowledge. In L. Lemieux-Charles & F. Champagne (Eds.). *Using Knowledge and*

Evidence in Health Care: Multidisciplinary Perspectives (pp. 18-40). Toronto: University of Toronto Press.

Doel, M. & Penn, J. (2007). Technical assistance, neo-colonialism or mutual trade? The experience of an Anglo/Ukrainian/Russian social work practice learning projects. *European Journal of Social Work*, 10 (3), 367-381.

Freed, A.O. (1995). Bulgarian social services and social work education. *International Social Work, 38*, 39-51.

George, J. (1999). Conceptual muddle, practical dilemma: Human rights, social development and social work education. *International Social Work, 42*, 15-26.

Gray, M. & Fook, J. (2004). The quest for a universal social work: Some issues and implications. *Social Work Education, 23(5)*, 625–644.

Gray, M. & Simpson, B. (1998). Developmental social work education: A field example. *International Social Work, 41*, 227-237.

Hrycak, A. (2002). From mothers' rights to equal rights. In N.A. Naples & M. Desai (Eds.) *Women's Activism and Globalization*, (pp. 64-82). New York: Routledge.

Iarskaia-Smirnova, E. & Romanov, P. (2002). A salary is not important here: The professionalization of social work in contemporary Russia. *Social Policy & Administration*, 36(2), 123-141.

Iarskaia-Smirnova, E., Romanov, P. & Lovtsova, N. (2004). Professional development of social work in Russia. *Social Work & Society*, 2(1), 132-138.

Iarskaia-Smirnova, E. & Romanov, P. (2008). Gendering social work in Russia: towards anti-discriminatory practices. *Equal Opportunities International*, 27(1), 64-76.

Kolb, D. (1984). *Experiential Learning: Experience as the Source of Learning and Development.* Englewood Cliffs, N.J: Prentice-Hall.

Kolkov, V., Shapiro, B., & Solovyov, A. (2000). Managing the development of social work in Russia. In E. Harlow & J. Lawler (Eds.) *Management, Social Work and Change* (pp. 133-166). Aldershot, UK: Ashgate.

Kurland, R. & Salmon, R. (1998). *Teaching a Methods Course in Social ?Work with Groups.* Alexandria, VA: CSWE.

Mesbur, E.S. and Glassman, U. (1991). From commitment to curriculum: The humanistic foundations of field instruction. In D. Schneck, B. Grossman, & U. Glassman (Eds.). *Field Education in Social Work: Contemporary Issues and Trends* (pp. 47-58). Dubuque, Iowa: Kendall/Hunt.

Penn, J. (2007). The development of social work education in Russia since 1995. *European Journal of Social Work*, 10(4), 513-527.

Payne, M. (1991). *Modern Social Work Theory: A Critical Introduction.* London: Macmillan Press.

Rutgers University Center for International Social Work. (2008). *Social Work Education and the Practice Environment in Europe and Eurasia.* Report produced for the Social Transition Team, Office of Democracy, Governance and Social Transition of the United States Agency for International Development. Retrieved on 20 August 2010 from www.usaid.gov/ locations/ europe_eurasia/dem_gov/docs/ best_practice_in_social_work_final_121008.pdf.

Schwartz, W. (1960). *Content and Process in the Educative Experience.* Unpublished dissertation, Columbia University.

Schwartz, W. (1980). Education in the classroom. *Journal of Higher Education,* 51(3), 235-254.

Shulman, L. (1970). The hidden group in the classroom. *Learning and Development, 2,* 1-6.

Somers, M.L. (1971). Dimensions and dynamics of engaging the learner. *Journal of Education for Social Work,* 5(2), 61-73.

Taylor, Z. (1999). Values, theories and methods in social work education: A culturally transferable core? *International Social Work,* 42(3), 309-318.

Templeman, S.B. (2001). Social work in the new Russia at the start of the millennium. *International Social Work* 47(1), 95-107.

Torres, R.-M. (2001). Knowledge-based international aid. Do we want it, do we need it?' In W. Gmelin, K. King, & S. McGrath (Eds), *Development Knowledge, National Research and International Cooperation* (pp. 103-124). University of Edinburgh. CAS-DSE-NORRAG, Edinburgh, Bonn, Geneva.

Tunney, K. (2002). Learning to teach abroad: Reflections on the role of the visiting social work educator. *International Social Work,* 45(4), 435-446.

Trygged, S. & Eriksson, B. (2009). Implementing Swedish models of social work in a Russian context. *Social Work & Society,* 7(2), 273-284.

Whitmore, E. & M. Wilson (1997). Accompanying the process: Social work and international development practice. *International Social Work, 40,* 57-74.

5
The facilitator 411 on phone groups:
When caller ID isn't enough
Vicki Hallas

Summary

The purpose of this paper is to illustrate the challenges presented while facilitating a national, 12-week telephone support group (TSG) for women diagnosed with ovarian cancer as a second year student in field placement. Special emphasis is given to the struggles students encounter when applying face-to-face, visual-based skills to auditory practice (Middleman & Wood, 1990). Importance is given to Stage Development theory and the role of Screening. Close attention is paid to the challenges Cognitive and Perception skills pose for non-visual groups (Middleman & Wood, 1990). Delineated group work skills are taken from Middleman & Wood (1990).

Introduction

Seasoned workers with years of practice tend to glorify the Telephone Support Group (TSG) experience by reiterating their numerous rewards (Evans, Halar, and Smith, 1985; Napolitano, Babyak, Palmer, Tapson, Davis and Blumenthal, 2006). This can be daunting for students who feel insecure or embarrassed by their multiple mishaps. Suddenly, basic skills, once taken for granted, such as *looking with planned emptiness* and *zooming* can be strenuous (Middleman & Wood, 1990); while more advanced techniques, like *looking from diverse angles* and *using a wide-angle lens* (Middleman & Wood, 1990) seem unfeasible. So if and 'when groups go wrong', this passed-on wisdom may become frustrating (Schopler & Galinsky, 1981, p. 424). Such frustration is resonated in Schopler, Galinsky, and Abell (1997), who candidly state: 'professionals reporting on their own innovative practice tend to emphasize the positive aspects of telephone and computer groups. They are less likely to discuss the risks and ineffective interventions related to the use of technology' (Schopler, Galinsky, & Abell, 1997, p. 21).

This paper will report on some of the not-so-positive aspects of facilitating a national, 12-week TSG for seven women between the ages of 46-76 diagnosed with ovarian cancer as a second-year student in field placement. By elaborating on the risks and ineffective interventions, it is hoped that effective interventions are illustrated.

When inquiring about TSG literature, I was informed that there was 'not much out there'. Yet, an employee who worked at the same agency had published two poignant articles on technology-based groups.

Review of the literature

The call for additional TSGs in social service agencies literally rings true. With the increasing need for technology-based groups comes the increasing demand for skilled workers. Much literature has been published by professionals on the efficacy of TSGs connecting clients otherwise unable to attend traditional face-to-face groups, such as the elderly, immobile, or sick (Goelitz, 2003; Goodman & Pynoos, 1990; Meier, Galinsky, & Rounds, 1995; Rittner & Hammons, 1992). Learning what past practitioners willingly share serves as a fulcrum for future practice (Rounds, Galinsky & Despard, 1995).

TSG literature may be the only resource for students in search of supervision and support (Goelitz, 2004; Rounds, Galinsky, & Stevens, 1991; Smith, Toseland, Rizzo, & Zinoman, 2004). Initially, fledgling facilitators flustered by either lack of training at field work or instruction in coursework may find reading these successes extremely helpful (Schopler, Abell, & Galinsky, 1998). These works often explore the struggles that facilitators encounter during preliminary phases of setting up and of using technology (Evans & Jauregay, 1981; Nokes, Chew, & Altman, 2003; Thomas & Urbano, 1993). Many articles offer useful strategies to consider in planning stages (Lester & Thomas, 2002; Spiegel & Classen, 2000). Such accounts are essential references in delineating how to apply ostensibly visual 'face-to-face' group work skills based on reading facial cues and body language (such as *scanning, positioning,* and *attending*) to non-visual, auditory methods for over-the-phone practice (Colon, 1996; Middleman & Wood, 1990). Most articles acknowledge the hardship that rudimentary facilitators endure (Galinsky, Schopler & Abell, 1997; Shepard, 1987). Frequently, however, the message is one of reassurance and concluding that benefits outweigh drawbacks for members and facilitators alike. With little else, the guidance and assistance shared by polished professionals is appreciated, especially when field work supervisors are unaware of its existence (Brown, Pain, Berwald, Hirschi, Delehanty, & Miller, 1999; Colon, 1996; Evans, Fox, Pritzl, & Halar, 1984; Stein, Rothman, & Nakanishi, 1993; Weiner, Dupont Spence, Davidson, & Fair, 1993).

Agency avoidance

My field placement was at a non-profit, privately funded organization offering financial and legal assistance, as well as *gratis* group and individual counseling to those affected by cancer and their families. Starting off primarily to serve local New Yorkers in person, the advent of technology-based supportive services reached national and international contingents. Pivoting back to the late 1980s, this agency soon became a juggernaut in the field.

For the student intern, an oncology field work placement can be both rigorous and rewarding. Succinct in nature, mandated training and supervision revolved around diagnosis, treatment, and prognosis lasting the entire academic year. Cancer type and stage along with physical and emotional side effects were parsed. Basically, student presence was valued, and one left with a treasure trove of knowledge; so it was uncanny when the topic of group work was broached and an unsettling ellipsis filled the air. Various articles were disseminated as material to be 'reviewed at home' or 'on the subway,' the bulk of which included a phalanx of antiquated directions on opening a telephone account. Answering the outcry of interns begging for instruction on '*running* a telephone support group,' one speaker addressed this topic in 15-minutes (Middleman & Wood, 1990), during which appreciation of phone groups was expressed with a light-hearted chuckle, 'you can do other things while on the phone,' and 'don't worry, no one can see how nervous you are!' One handout outlined a group seating chart: circles in different sizes and shapes represented group members encompassing one larger oblong symbolizing the facilitator. Explained as a 'crucial part' of the orientation packet, it was to be mailed-out to TSG members so that they could create a 'visual image to the voice on the other end of the receiver,' as members '*need* to know what one another look like.'

Since terminal illness and end-of-life issues in conjunction to group work and technology-based groups were unfamiliar terrain, student panic erupted. A plea was compiled in the form of an inquiry: 'Interns co-facilitate with a supervisor, *right*?' Our desperation went unnoticed, and a rebuttal ('Students facilitate *alone* for a better learning experience') only led to complete hysteria. Strangely, staff co-facilitated but not with interns. Interns did not even co-facilitate with other interns. I blurted out, 'What if we're sick?' The response was greeted coldly with a blank stare and a perplexed, 'That hasn't happened here.' (In an agency dealing with cancer focusing on death and dying—offering numerous groups for over 20 years—employees do not get sick? They clearly did, for agency protocol listed an employee sick-line!). Interestingly, three interns out of five became severely ill for longer than six weeks, one of whom developed shingles and losing facial functioning on one side of his face. The 15 minutes ended with a caveat on limited office space available and reservations for face-to-face groups. There was no mention of TSGs or the 'reservation only' requirement.

Facilitator freak-out:
Phone-friendly or fearful?

When three interns were assigned TSGs, anxiety heightened. I was the only student who had worked with groups prior, but that said, I somehow felt resentful: *Of all the gin joints in all the towns in all the world, I walk into this one. Moi,* a phone group at Rick's Café! Can't they give it to Frenchie at the bar? I perceived telephone work as purgatory. Group work was sexy—a phone group was NOT! What would we do? Who would we look at? I sighed, 'this is the last thing I *need!'*

When telling friends of my phone fear, they burst out laughing and hollered, 'Oh, so now the big mouth with a busy signal has nothing to say?' It was true; I was on the telephone incessantly. My first childhood toy was a play-phone. You pressed 0 and a doll-like operator popped out singing a tune. However, when I told my peers about my 'facilitator freak-out,' they burst out sobbing in my face, railing, 'At least you've *done* groups. This is my first group ever!' One intern hissed, 'They talk about secondary trauma? I've got TSG trauma!'

Apparitions of myself roaming down a long, dark hallway with the lights flickering on and off surface with strange moans, shrieks, and wails in the background. The hallway elongates with each step - never ending. Limping, I feel someone following me. I imagine Hitchcock's 'Dial M for Murder' and get goose bumps. Shivering, I come upon a dusty, dingy barren room with nothing but a mammoth Commissioner Gordon-like red Batphone —looming, lop-sided on the floor—a rotary succubus. The foreign-like apparatus startles me with its piercing ring. Trembling, I pick-it-up. The voice on the other end identifies himself as a police officer who barrels, 'Ma'am, we've traced the calls; they're coming from inside the house!'

I was not alone in my real-life episode of 'When A Stranger Calls.' The other interns were right there with me scrambling to escape. One student ailing with phone-fright procrastinated for so long that she almost lost her placement. In fact, I was the only intern to promptly start and complete a TSG.

Screening sight from sound

Pregroup interviews are used for two purposes: to make an assessment of a prospective group member and to prepare that person for entry in the group. The two purposes might be addressed in a single pregroup interview or they might be done in separate meetings. (Northen & Kurland, 2001, p. 166)

Eyes rolled as I spent more time screening than the agency thought that a 'good clinician' should (10-minutes). Often, 'client requested group' was a *fait accompli* guaranteeing membership. TSG screenings were similar to if not longer than my face-to-face pregroup contact: 45-minutes.

The longer you spend screening, however, the less you spend deciphering a member's voice, silence, and sorrow. In the case of terminal illness, whose chuckle belongs to whom and whose cry doesn't become vital to know. The recognition of lulls, laughter, and lachrymose is paramount. It *may* be hurtful for the group if the facilitator is struggling with who is speaking in the beginning stage (Garland, Jones & Kolodny, 1973); but it surely *will* be damaging for the group if the facilitator is still struggling with who is crying in the ending stage (Garland, Jones, & Kolodny, 1973).

Telephone work is a different culture. The language and customs have to be learned. My native tongue was face-to-face dialogue. I was fluent in face-*glish*. Half the battle in learning a second language is acquainting one's ear to the rhythm. Screenings offer facilitators an Immersion 101 course. TSG facilitators focus on cadence and intonation. Speech patterns set the stage for *positioning* and *attending* skills (Middleman & Wood, 1990). Rather than *scanning* what appears to be, *continuous group* skills hone in on what *sounds* to be; thus, 'You look upset' becomes 'You sound upset.' Sound consists of melody. Screening is your Caller ID: it is the 411-metronome pacing you through the score of possible disharmony.

'The benefits of pregroup interviews to prepare clients for participation in a group have been well established' (Northen & Kurland, 2001, p. 167). For telephone groups, screening is a chance for members to express their own phone fear and anxiety about the unknown, possibly putting the facilitator at ease. When screening, the following concerns were raised:

Member #1: *I just don't get it. How does this work if we can't see each other?*

Member #2: *I'm nervous. How do we know who's speaking?*

Member #3*: I'm worried about interrupting someone. Won't we all interrupt each other?*

Facilitators can respond by *running out alternatives* and *pointing out possible consequences* (Middleman & Wood, 1990). TSG format can request members to announce their names prior to speaking until everyone recognizes everyone else. Admitting that group members may interrupt each other *universalizes the issue* (Middleman & Wood, 1990).

Interruptions of course occur in any conversation, and interrupting confuses things. At first, I tried to pretend it would never happen; then, I tried to pretend it would never happen *to me*. Ultimately, when it did happen, *reporting on my own feelings* of confusion normalized the situation and assuaged members' fears (Middleman & Wood, 1990). *Summarizing difficulty* (Middleman & Wood, 1990) embraced confusion and candor. Discussing interruptions helped to *confront distortions* and to *give feedback* (Middleman & Wood, 1990). *Connecting the new to the known* permitted members to *report on feelings* and to *build on group* (Middleman & Wood, 1990). Interruptions may even be desired as conflict occurs, furnishing an opportunity to *further group cohesion* and voice group achievement (Middleman & Wood, 1990).

Yet, much of the time students were so rushed to start groups due to the pressure of class assignments and agency demands that this opportunity for screening was purloined. Interns were cornered into accepting inappropriate members encountered unfortunate results. Groups that consisted of members with issues other than cancer thwarted group need, purpose and dynamic. 'Clients will stop coming and a group will disintegrate if members view the group as unconnected to their real needs and interests' (Northen & Kurland, 2001, p. 176). When membership wanes as members *do* leave, the few members remaining rarely benefit. A redux of two group members total (couples therapy?) was referred to as 'grouplettes' and encouraged, adding to facilitator stress. For example, one intern was forced to start a TSG immediately and in haste accepted a victim of domestic violence. During one group session, this member's husband grabbed the phone and threatened the facilitator and members alike, ending the group at session six, when only two members called in.

The silent screen

Special attention to silence(s) during screenings and throughout group stages should be paid. Silences ebb and flow conversations. Yet, respites tend to evoke discomfort, especially if you cannot see them. Silences should be acknowledged and explored. In end-of-life work silences may scream out pain, tears, or sadness. With caution, skills applied to silences can be *reaching for* or *waiting out feelings* (Middleman & Wood, 1990). If facilitators observe members struggling with silence, they can *invite full participation* or *turn issues back to group* (Middleman & Wood, 1990). Silences that fall on a facilitator's deaf ear simply hinder group development.

Phone faux pas

Screening is a time to address the issue of background or unforeseen noise. Facilitators should think about the people they speak with on-the-phone and those to whom they would rather not and *why*. TSG etiquette and phone *faux pas* can be addressed in screenings by *inviting full participation* or *turning back to the group* (Middleman & Wood, 1990) in the beginning stage (Garland, Jones, & Kolodny, 1973) or by *verbalizing norms* (Middleman & Wood, 1990).

In my experience, speaker phones and cell phones did not work well – especially, when used in public places, although in one case a member asked the group if she could use her cell phone while driving long distance for Thanksgiving; members agreed, and it worked out nicely. The group also allowed another member to use her cell phone while waiting for chemotherapy in the hospital; this too was fine. Radios, television, or other background noise was not, while typing, eating, cooking or cleaning caused overt friction. Fortunately, our subcontracted agency had the sophistication to allow callers to temporarily cease their call-waiting and block-out noise, which meant they could hear us, but we could not hear them. Other unforeseen noise included construction, traffic, deliveries, and dogs. In such cases facilitators may *recast problems*, *run out alternatives*, or *give feedback* (Middleman & Wood, 1990); while *selecting communication patterns purposefully* helps members to *reinforce group norms* (Middleman and Wood, 1990).

TSGs do not meet in private spaces with the proverbial office-door-shut, which possibly forfeits a sense of structure or professionalism. Such casualness may expedite honesty and intimacy, but it may also inhibit confidentiality. TSGs may result in the work not being valued by either members or agency. Members who have young children and family in the home during group have to make a commitment to rules, which may be difficult for some members of oncology groups where a caretaker or visiting nurse is required. A 'group room of one's own,' where the door can be closed without interruption is vital (Woolf, 1981). In my experience, some members were employed; some took care of an elderly parent; some had a caretaker; and for some this meant declining participation while for others, it meant adjustments. My group permitted a visiting nurse; a member with an elderly parent used a separate room; the working- professional member had enough status to shut her office door without disruption.

Like face-to-face groups, TSGs are handled *seriously*, a seriousness that holds doubly true for agencies. At our placement, my co-interns struggled equally to find a room of their own, and as we could not reserve office space for TSGs, we embarked on a treasure hunt of 'X marks-the-spot. A big round circle with a tiny, little dot,' which led us to haphazardly scavenge empty offices. Hesitant was the staff member who found his or her office trespassed upon by TSG intern squatters. Under the impression that students absconded into private offices to make personal phone calls on company time, administrators knocked ferociously or transferred calls incessantly. I shared my office with three other interns, which became tedious. On a day when my presence was required at school for Common Day, my dedication was questioned when I wanted to reschedule the group, as I could use a cell phone 'from the cafeteria' or 'even outside if it was a nice day to *run* group.' Flummoxed, I admitted to not owning a cell phone, to which the response was that I might use '*any* street corner pay phone.' Thus may TSG facilitators encounter agency disregard for the work and the worker.

When cancer calls

TSG facilitators should know the limitations of their members, because agency assumptions can be misleading. Chemotherapy and radiation treatment(s) often cause debilitating nausea, diarrhea, and sickness as well as peripheral neuropathy (Hartman & Loprinzi, 2005). In my group sudden sickness forced members to excuse themselves to go the bathroom, putting the phone down temporarily and returning later or hanging up altogether. *Running out alternatives* (Middleman &Wood, 1990), the group voiced compassion for both circumstances. Medications can cause drowsiness. For example, one member fell asleep on the phone twice. *Turning issues back to group* (Middleman & Wood, 1990), members decided to 'just let the woman rest.' Embarrassed by her drowsiness, she was comforted by the group, which stated, 'This is *our* reality.' Neuropathy infers the loss of equilibrium, causing vertigo from severe numbing in hands and feet. Falling can debilitate members; facial injury after a fall impairs speech. Members may lisp or speak inaudibly. (I was told to reject clients with speech impediments based on 'past agency expertise.')

One screening revealed a potential member's stutter and slurred speech. A neuropathic-induced fall injured and bruised one side of her face, and a diabetic stroke permanently paralyzed the other. Diabetes took her right leg above the knee, and she was wheelchair dependent, living in a walk-up building on the Lower East Side of Manhattan. She rarely left her apartment, was completely isolated and lonely, and had six months of life expectancy. However, 'poor enunciation' made her an 'inappropriate fit,' and I was advised to 'deny group access.' *Immediately*, I invited her to join the group. In fact, she was the first person I accepted. A *tour de force*, she was the most active and courageous member -- the first to verbalize fears on dying... and everyone understood her just fine!

Furthermore, funding stipulations often assign TSG purpose. Unaware of the nature and magnitude of the work, over-emphasis on TSG 'benefits' was prevalent. The assigned purpose of my group was 'to support patients during the holidays.' As a student, I was not scheduled to be in placement over the holidays... but as an intern I *was* expected to hold group from wherever I was, because I could 'call in from any location... *even* on safari!' – an expectation that was tossed around as one of the many TSG 'benefits.' On the other hand, during a New York City transit strike I did call from home, and the group was extremely grateful.

Saving face in ſtage development

Slightly altering stage development theory (Garland, Jones, & Kolodny,

1973) is a more profound facilitator role in all TSG stages. Face-to-face group facilitator presence is pendulous, swinging strong in beginnings and again at endings (Northen & Kurland, 2001), so the longitude of TSG facilitator presence within all three stages including middles can be confounding. Therefore, precisely because facilitator presence cannot be seen, it should be heard—even in middles; and so in my group, unlike in my face-to-face work, my voice and role continued throughout all stages. So that members know you are present, you play more of a beginnings role in middles. In visual practice members are reassured by sight; in auditory practice members are reassured by sound. Eye contact, nodding, and other facial cues normally used in visual *scanning, attending,* and *positioning* are replaced with verbal ones such as, 'mmm,' 'ah-hah' or the occasional, 'right' and 'yes.' Paradoxically, however, TSG facilitator presence in all stages makes members comfortable and facilitators uncomfortable, because it differs from taught visual methodology (Garland, Jones, & Kolodny, 1973; Northen & Kurland, 2001). However, saving face in stage development is the facilitator's flexibility from beginnings to endings.

Phone fiasco: Just a phone-call away

When TSGs are utilized clients tend to consider clinicians 'just a phone-call away.' This can sometimes lead to unwarranted communication from members outside of group, increasing worker stress and phone fiascos. If facilitators screen over the telephone, and the group is over the telephone, members tend to call in between group sessions. When agency policies are not initially clarified or later rectified, facilitators may want to disconnect completely from what is referred to as 'off-the-hook' work.

Contradicting agency phone and face-to-face group counseling procedures make things even more trying. In my internship face-to-face groups assigned each member a social worker (other than the facilitator) to handle case-management concerns for the duration of the group. TSG members were not assigned such a worker. Jettisoned, some members relied on facilitators for case management while others did not, dividing the group and resulting in an armada of calls throughout the week, causing some to become subjected to role lock as monopolizers, scapegoats, mistrusters, or isolates (Bogdanoff & Elbaum, 1978). No doubt, agency disregard or complete lack of proper protocol for TSGs create additional stress for facilitators and members.

My mistake began by not *establishing rules* or *setting limits* (Middleman & Wood, 1990) as to the frequency and purpose of contact outside of group, which blew up in my face as members were, as the RAP song shouts, 'blowing-up my pager.' There was one member whose group attendance was irregular. She resided in Canada and had forgotten the U.S. Martin Luther King holiday. Knowing I handled case management concerns for some group members, she contacted me and was soon upset at my reticence to engage. Enraged, she left the group. The next group session was suddenly interrupted by a crank-caller who entered the line unannounced to blast Beethoven's Fifth Symphony, impairing the group from hearing. Completely startled, I found myself shouting uncontrollably, 'HANG-UP AND JUST CALL BACK!' At the following session it happened again, and the group mentioned this member's penchant for classical music. I called the TSG subcontractor, who suggested a caller-block option and the crank-call *symphonies* ceased. Frankly, however, I was upset: if policies had been clearly implemented for telephone groups, none of this might have happened. Fortunately, my outrage influenced TSG agency procedure so that currently, all TSG members are assigned social workers.

Need not, want not: Facilitator vs. group need

> If need is not recognized and acknowledged by the members of a group, then that group's purpose is apt to have little meaning for its members and the likelihood is that the group will fail. It is essential that a group's purpose be connected integrally to members' perceptions of what they want and need. (Northen & Kurland, 2001, p.176)

My own facilitator-fear combined with agency misgivings hindered my understanding of group need and purpose as I obsessed about my own. If I could only *see* the group, this group would not 'go wrong' (Schopler & Galinsky, 1981). Our training indicated that group members *needed* to know what everyone *looked* liked, so I mailed-out the orientation packets that included the seating chart diagram, my nemesis.

But I became my biggest nemesis from the beginning: I thought I knew member needs. I did not. Patients living in rural areas commonly traveled up to 150 miles each way to the nearest hospital. Daily chemotherapy or radiation treatment(s) made for physically and financially arduous commutes. Unable to drive and the soaring cost of gas stymied treatment altogether. Some were fortunate enough to eschew losing employment, filing for bankruptcy and relocating entirely. One member shared the lack of group availability stating, 'In Utah, the only support group is the extended family—and it's already been done *extended*!' Another member moved to Atlanta for one of the best gynecological oncology units in the country but conveyed, 'Groups are good if you have breast cancer. No one's even heard of an ovarian group out here.'

For the first session I reviewed their packets and addressed questions. Members found the phone system user friendly, contradicting much of the literature (Smith, Toseland, Rizzo, & Zinoman, 2004). Then I perused the seating chart, which was dictated as a good introductory exercise, because members *needed* to 'put a visual to voice.' But, being 'looked at' when one had just lost their hair, eyebrows, and eye lashes was disconcerting (Middleman & Wood, 1990, p. 21) after having their ovaries, uterus, colon, or other internal organs removed and external appendices inserted, such as a peg or ostomy bag, is troublesome. If this includes surgical scarring or bulking and treatment or steroid weight gain, it is detrimental (Hartman & Loprinzi, 2005). Dangerous cell histology and advanced site malignancy may result in 'catastrophic surgery,' such as 'clearance of the abdominal cavity' or 'vulva excision' (Burton & Watson, 1988, p. 58). One member complaining of stomach pain for a year was prescribed to 'diet.' Walking into the emergency room with presumed indigestion, she left six weeks later in a wheelchair. A ruptured hernia operation detected the spread of late stage ovarian cancer resulting in the removal of abdominal cavities. Surgical complications resulted in a botched, narrowly-sutured colostomy obstructing bowel functioning. Disfiguring deformity and morbid abdominal swelling paralyzed her. As 'interference with bowel function' is 'the most common cause of death from ovarian cancer,' members rallied in support enabling her to pursue corrective, exigent surgery (Hartman & Loprinzi, 2005, p. 339).

Inherently, being 'looked at' was equated with judgment (Middleman & Wood, 1990), so that the TSG provided a protective safe environment. Without being 'looked at' members could truly be *seen* apart from their physical appearance (Middleman & Wood, 1990). One member upset by her hair loss later conveyed, 'I refuse to let my husband of 27 years look at me without a wig. I sleep with it on!' The group was not ready to divulge what had previously stigmatized them, so as they hesitated a long awkward silence evolved. *Phone failure!* The member who had a speech impediment and amputated leg saved the day. Feeling as if her 'voice' already sketched a biased 'visual,' she intercepted with strength, grace, and humor, breaking the tension with, 'Everyone says I'm so brave, but I would like to see them walk just one mile in my SHOE. And SHOE, ladies, are my weakness—let them try walking in my ONE stiletto, sneaker, or ballet slipper! ... Not only do I look like Rocky Balboa, I sound like him, too! I hope that's OK.' Members, utterly relieved, quickly joined in to thank her, sharing their own 'phone-voice' discontent as they exaggerated their Southern or Midwestern accents.

Skill oversight: Seeing sound

Once acclimated to phone work, cognitive skills such as *recognizing feelings, connecting the new to the known,* and *reflecting on the work* (Middleman & Wood, 1990) became easier -- easier than *perception skills,* for example, because cognition infers awareness and knowing whereas perception infers vision and discernment. Perception skills (Middleman & Wood, 1990), listed as *looking with planned emptiness, looking from diverse angles,* and *using a wide-angle lens,* seemed more difficult on the telephone, because technically, there was nothing to 'look at' (Middleman & Wood, 1990)... *Or was there?* Middleman and Wood (1990) discuss such myopia, contending that :

> We can look at something and not really *see* it! What we (decide to) *see* depends upon our mental readiness...that lead us to notice certain particulars of the 'seen' (the scene) and to accord importance to these particulars. (p. 21)

Seeing sound was a frequent skill oversight. Sight incorporates the facilitator's willingness to observe the whole picture: the entire person. Blinded, I envisioned perception skills as impossible or 'ineffective' (Schopler, Galinsky, & Abell, 1997). Without being able to *look at* everything, I was able *to see* something; focusing on sound made my practice more comprehensive. For example, *looking with planned emptiness* consisted of 'How are you right now?' *Looking from diverse angles* became 'Is there another option that comes to mind?' *Using a wide-angle lens* was 'A few sessions ago you would have... , and now you have the courage to...'

Simultaneously, TSG facilitators should tune in to a 'listening vs. hearing' methodology, as Middleman and Wood (1990) suggest:

> Listening is comparable to looking; hearing comparable to seeing. To really hear is quite different from mere listening. One can listen but not hear. *Hearing* is the outcome of listening, just as *seeing* is the outcome of looking. To *hear* demands active attention devoted to dealing with the words that the brain receives, sorting through and selecting the key, meaningful words or themes. (p. 21)

In visual practice *listening* rather than *hearing* may be automatic. In contrast, auditory work amplifies *hearing* rather than *listening*, because sight is veiled and so sound is revealed. Essentially, 'I hear you' is the same as 'I see you,' because it means 'I understand you.'

Ultimately, 'ineffective interventions' are effective if facilitators dare to 'risk' making, 'reporting,' and sharing them (Schopler, Galinsky, & Abell, 1997, p. 21). Taking risks insinuates risking yourself and your practice—*for a better one.*

Conclusion

When the group ended members requested another TSG and continued to communicate with one another by calling and emailing each other—even sending photographs. Those who lived in neighboring states planned to travel for face-to-face visits. A reunion in Dallas for the Women's Gynecological Cancer Foundation Conference (2006) was being organized, and one member opened her home to house the entire group for a week. Other members raised funds and donated the money to airline tickets for those who could not afford it. Being *looked* at face-to-face for most of their diagnosis, members felt truly *seen* over-the-phone. *Listening* to all of this, I could not believe what I was *hearing.* I only wish, you could have *seen it.*

References

Bogdanoff, M. & Elbaum, P. (1978). Role lock: Dealing with monopolizers, mistrusters, isolates, helpful hannahs, and other assorted characters in group psychotherapy. *International Journal of Group Psychotherapy*, Vol. 18; 247-262.

Brown, R., Pain, K., Berwald, C., Hirschi, P., Delehanty, R. & Miller, H. (1999). Distance education and caregiver support groups: Comparison of traditional telephone groups. *The Journal of Head Trauma Rehabilitation*, 14(3), 257-268.

Burton, M. & Watson, M. (1988). *Counseling People with Cancer.* London, UK: John Wiley and Sons.

Colon, Y. (1996) Telephone support groups. *Cancer Practice*, 4(3), 156-159.

Evans, R., Fox, H., Pritzl, D., & Halar, E. (1984). Group treatment of physically disabled adults by telephone. *Social Work in Health Care*, 9(3), 77-84.

Evans, R., Halar, E., & Smith, K.(1985). Cognitive therapy to achieve personal goals: Results of telephone group counseling with disabled adults. *Archives of Physical and Medical Rehabilitation*, 66, 693-696.

Evans, R. & Jauregay, B.(1981). Group therapy by phone: A cognitive behavioral program for visually impaired elderly. *Social Work in Health Care*, 7(2), 79-91.

Galinsky, M., Schopler, J., & Abell, M.(1997). Connecting group members through telephone and computer groups. *Health and Social Work*, 22(3), 181-189.

Garland, J., Jones, H., & Kolodny, R. (1973). A model for stages in development in social work with groups,' in S. Bernstein (Ed.), *Explorations in Group Work* (pp. 17-71). Boston: Milford House.

Goelitz, A. (2004). Using the end of groups as an intervention at end-of-life. In R.Salmon & R. Graziano (Eds.), *Group Work and Aging* (pp. 211-221). Binghamton, NY: Haworth Press.

Goelitz, A. (2003). When accessibility is an issue: Telephone support groups for caregivers. *Smiith College Studies in Social Work*, 73 (3), 385-394.

Goodman, C.& Pynoos, J. (1990). A model telephone information and support program for caregivers of Alzheimer's patients. *The Gerontologist*, 30 (3), 399-404.

Hartman, L. & Loprinzi, C. (Eds.) (2005). *Mayo Clinic: Guide to Women's Cancers.* New York: Kensington Publishing Corporation.

Kurland, R., & Salmon, R. (2009). Caught in the doorway between education and practice: Group work's battle for survival. In C. Cohen, M.H. Phillips & M. Hanson (Eds)., *Strength and Diversity in Social Work with Groups*

(p. 11-21). New York: Routledge.

Lester, D. & Thomas, C. (2002). *Crisis Intervention and Counseling by Telephone.* Springfield, IL: Publisher, Ltd.

Malekoff, A. (2004). *Group Work With Adolescents.* (2nd ed.). New York: Guilford Press.

Meier, A., Galinsky, M., & Rounds, K.(1995). Telephone support groups for caregivers of persons with Aids. In M. Galinsky & J. Schopler (Eds.), *Support Groups* (pp. 99-108). Binghamton, NY: Haworth Press.

Middleman, R. & Wood, G. (1990). *Skills for Direct Practice in Social Work*: New York: Columbia University Press.

Napolitano, M., Babyak, M., Palmer, S., Tapson, V., Davis, R., & Blumenthal, J. (2006). Effects of a telephone-based psychosocial intervention for patients awaiting lung transplantation. *CHEST,* 122, 1176-1184.

Nokes, K., Chew, L., & Altman, C. (2003). Using a telephone support group for HIV-Positive persons aged 50+ to increase social support and health-related knowledge. *AIDS Patient Care and STDs,* 17(7), 345-351.

Northen, H. & Kurland, R. (2001). *Social Work with Groups.* New York: Columbia University Press.

Rittner, B., & Hammons, K. (1992). Telephone group work with people with end stage AIDS. *Social Work with Groups,* 15(4), 59-72.

Rounds, K., Galinsky, M., & Despard, M. (1995). Evaluation of telephone support groups for persons with HIV Disease. *Research on Social Work Practice,* 5(4), 442-459.

Rounds, K., Galinsky, M., & Stevens, L. (1991). Linking people with AIDS in rural communities: The telephone group. *Social Work,* 36(1), 13-18.

Schopler, J. & Galinsky, M.J. (1981). When groups go wrong. *Social Work,* 26(5), 424-429.

Schopler, J., Abell, M., & Galinsky, M. (1998). Technology-Based groups: A review and conceptual framework for practice. *Social Work,* 43(3), 254-267.

Schopler, J., Galinsky, M., & Abell, M. (1997). Creating community through telephone and computer groups: Theoretical and practice perspectives. *Social Work with Groups,* 20(40), 19-35.

Shepard, P. (1987). Telephone therapy: An alternative to isolation. Clinical Social Work, 15(1), 56-65.

Smith, T., Toseland, R., Rizzo, V., & Zinoman, M. (2004). In R. Salmon & R Graziano (Eds.), *Group Work and Aging* (pp.151-172). Binghamton, New York: Haworth Press.

Spiegel, D. & Classen, C. (2000). *Group Therapy for Cancer Patients.* New York: Basic Books Publication

Stein, L., Rothman, B., & Nakanishi, M. (1993). The telephone group:

Accessing group service to the homebound. *Social Work with Groups,* 16(1/2), 203-215.

Thomas, T. & Urbano, J. (1993). A telephone group support program for the visually-impaired elderly. *Clinical Gerontologist,* 13(2), 61-71.

Weiner, L., Dupont Spencer, E., Davidson, R., & Fair, C. (1993). National telephone support groups: A new avenue toward psychosocial support for HIV-Infected children and their families. *Social Work with Groups,* 16(3), 55-71.

Woolf, V. (1981). *A Room of One's Own.* Orlando, Florida: Harcourt, Inc.

6
Groupwork researchers as 'temporary insiders'

Mark Doel and Kim Orchard

Summary

This paper aims to build the evidence base for groupwork through an exploration of the potential for participant observation in groups. The value of the participant observation method is considered by presenting the available literature and by analysing its use with a particular group. The group used as a case example is one for parents and carers experiencing difficulties with the behaviour of their adolescent children, and it illustrates both the dilemmas and the opportunities of participant observation. This group's structure is described in detail to provide the backcloth against which the observation took place and to link the process of participant evaluation with the specific detail of the group programme.

The paper develops a variant of the notion of the participant observer, in this case as an active temporary insider in the group, in which the process of independent evaluation by a person external to the group inevitably becomes part of the group process itself. There is discussion of how best to use this characteristic of participant observation, concluding with some guidelines emerging from the research. The guidance is intended to aid temporary insiders to provide independent evaluation and to build the evidence base. The paper is a collaboration between a groupwork academic and a groupwork practitioner.

Introduction

An evaluation of groupwork services was commissioned by South Gloucestershire Youth and Children's Services Department, a public agency in the English South Midlands. Included in this overall evaluation were observations of groups by the external researchers. This paper is the story of one of these participant observations. The group in question is a Parenting Skills group for parents and carers wanting to understand and manage the difficult behaviour of their adolescent children. The principles and practices of the groupwork are, therefore, different to those one might use in direct work with adolescents themselves (Malekoff, 2004).

The group which provides the illustration for the analysis in this paper is one supported by an Adolescent Support Team staffed by social workers and adolescent support workers. The team works with young people between the ages of 11 and 17 and one of the main aims is to support young people at home and to prevent them from being accommodated by the local authority (section 20, The Children Act 1989). Although the majority of the work is with young people and their families on a 'one-to-one' basis, the team has established a strong and regular groupwork service. The Managing Difficult Behaviour group is one of the groups which the team has offered on a regular basis for the past six years (24 different groups to date). There is a working plan for each session and details are provided later, though this is used very flexibly and the groups are *not* curriculum-driven. Immediately following the session, the facilitators meet to de-brief and evaluate. The participant observer took part in the debriefing following the session that was observed. The agency provides fortnightly supervision of groupwork for the three facilitators together.

The group

The purposes of the Managing Difficult Behaviour (MDB) groups are:

- to improve communication between parents/carers and adolescents
- to support and help group members to feel less isolated

- to develop a better understanding of adolescence and what 'positive parenting' can mean
- to consider rewards and sanctions and what works
- to know how to use the information and advice from the group

Referrals to the groups are made from a wide range of agencies such as youth offending and children's teams, health, education and police. Once a referral has been made, there is a one to one meeting with the prospective group member (or parenting couple) to consider whether groupwork is appropriate. The research suggests that this offer of groupwork on an individual basis is likely to encourage better attendance, by enabling mutual selection before the group first meets (Doel, 2006). The experience of the adolescent support team confirms this, with attendance and reliability increasing markedly since the pre-group interviews were instituted two years ago.

The Managing Difficult Behaviour (MDB) groups are typically composed of white women and men. Although over the 24 groups about 75% of members have been women, there has been a notable increase in men attending since the groupworkers started visiting group members in pre-group contacts, where they are able to discuss the importance of attendance by *both* parents or carers. There have been very few black members of the group and this reflects the local population. The age range of group members has been from 35 to 50 and typically late 30s. Three facilitators work with up to 15 parents and carers in each group. The group runs over 10 weekly evening sessions from 7.00 pm to 8.30 pm. However, members are encouraged to arrive at 6.30 pm to share refreshments and for 'chat time'. This gives members the chance to have non-threatening conversations and the session itself is rarely interrupted by late-comers. The refreshments are in a different room to the group meeting and this provides a natural break.

Parents and carers who attend the group often continue to meet up on their own to support each other after the ten sessions have finished. This is something that is encouraged early in the group by developing a contacts list ('Let's Keep In Touch') which group members can decide to sign up to, or decline. These continuation groups have proved successful in supporting group members to continue their problem solving without social work intervention. However, not every group decides to continue.

What people want from the group

Group members invariably start the group in a state of crisis, usually attending the first session with a feeling that they are alone with their problem. One of the most powerful aspects of the group is the discovery that they are not. A typical situation is described below:

> A referral is made by the parents with a request from them to have their young person accommodated by the local authority (taken out of the parents' care). The young person might even have been dropped off at social service offices and left. These situations will immediately activate support in the form of conflict resolution. The MDB group is offered as part of the support. When parents reach this stage they are often dealing with very extreme behaviours.
>
> Group members are asked to respond to some questions in writing before they come to the group. A questionnaire called Before the Group Begins is designed to help members to think about groups in general as well as this one in particular. It can be a useful focus for the individual pre-group meetings with prospective members and it provides a benchmark to measure change and indicate what, if any, part the group has played in these changes. These are the responses of one couple, Mandy and Richard (names have been anonymised).

Before the group begins ...
We are looking forward to the group and we hope that it will be useful and enjoyable for you. Before the group begins, it is very helpful if you can answer some questions. We will return to these at the end of the group and it will help you and us to know whether the group has been a success for you. Thank you.

Your name: *Mandy and Richard S*

How you would like to be called in the group? *as above*

Your age: *42 and 49*

1. **Have you been a member of a group before** (if yes, please say what kinds of group)? *Amateur dramatics, squash and badminton teams.*

2. **How did you get to know about this group?** *At a Family Support Meeting.*

3. **What do you want most of all from this group?** *Control and a normal family life.*

4. **Why do you think a group might be able to help?** *Other parents' ideas on how to manage [our son] George.*

5. **What will you bring to the group** (for example, a good sense of humour)? *Ideas and fun.*

6. **Do you have any concerns or worries about the group?** If so, what are these? *No.*

7. **When the group finishes in 10 weeks, what realistic changes would you like to see in your situation by then?** Please be specific. *That we deal with George in a consistent way.*

8. **Would it be OK to contact you after the group has finished?** Say six months later to find out how things are going for you? If yes, please let us have a contact address or number (of course, you can change your mind at any stage): *Yes.*

Mandy and Richard were unusual in making links with other activities and social groups (Q1), but this is useful to help people see this group experience in the context of others that may not have been perceived as 'groups'. It is common for people to be unsure how the group might help them (Q4) and new members need to be reassured that this is fine. Although Mandy and Richard had no worries about the group, some people express fears that they will be nervous, that they might talk too much or not enough, that they will not see a benefit, or they raise practical issues such as child minding costs. At this stage, before the group has begun, the realistic changes (Q7) tend to focus on the behaviour of the adolescent.

Many potential group members hope for skills to help them cope with the situation at home. They are looking for new ideas and, though professional help is mentioned, many are already alert to the opportunity for learning from other group members. Answering these questions before the group begins is designed to prompt people to start *thinking group.*

What happens in the group sessions

The Managing Difficult Behaviour group programmes have evolved over the six years through the experience of the groups themselves. This is an outline of the current pattern.

Sessional pattern

Before each session one of the three facilitators is available outside the building to greet members (and, for the first session, to show them where refreshments are). It is important to establish patterns in groups so that each session has a rhythm that is familiar. This establishes a reliable and safe environment and one in which the pattern can be deliberately changed in order to alter the rhythm (Doel, 2006). Of course, a pattern needs to be recognised as a pattern before it can be recognisably broken!

Except when people work in pairs or small groups, the group always sits in a circle, with the three facilitators distributed fairly evenly through the group. Sessions start with an Opening Circle, in which everyone has the opportunity to have a voice and offload how their week has been, scoring from one (very bad) to ten (extremely good). These scores are noted in order to monitor change and the group facilitators join in with this activity. Group members are introduced to a practice task in each group session, which they complete between one session and another. These are crucial for transferring learning from inside the group out to the home and community and to start to change feelings and behaviours. Finally, every session ends with a Closing Circle, in which the theme is always connected to adolescence, but in the context of the parents' own experiences of adolescence. For example, 'when you were a teenager what was your favourite music?' This has the dual purpose of taking group members back out into the world and also of putting them in touch with their own adolescence. As the group gains in confidence, members take turn to decide the adolescence topic for the Closing Circle and to lead it.

Session 1

The first session helps people get to know one another, covers house-keeping issues, considers the aims and objectives of the group and explores hopes and fears for the group. A Group Agreement is negotiated which incorporates all this and is available for the rest of the group as a guide and memo.

Session 2

The second session focuses on 'family mapping'. The group moves into three smaller groups each led by one of the facilitators and with the aim of exploring family dynamics via strengths (positives) and problems (issues). There are usually recurring and common issues within the group as a whole, which helps the leaders to anticipate likely themes and members to bond, by reinforcing the feeling that they are not alone with their problems.

Each person draws their family map (see figure 1 overleaf), with lines between family members representing the kind of relationship that they feel they have. They are asked to represent how problematic the relationship is by how zig-zag the line and the length of the line represents how close or distant they feel about their child. Other significant people can be added to the map. All the completed Family Mapping sheets are displayed up on the wall, which makes the similarities very graphic. This activity also gives the adolescents a kind of presence in the group.

Session 3

Adolescent development is the focus of this session. There is input about adolescent biology and psychology, such as brain development, risk taking and identity. The social aspects of adolescence ('what is it like for adolescents today?') are also introduced. The practice task for this session is a work sheet, the Stop-Think Circle in which the person completing the sheet records what they believe to be normal adolescent behaviour (in an outer circle) and what they identify as unacceptable behaviour (in an inner circle), with a suggestion that the questions 'Is it safe? Is it fair?' is used as guide.

Both group members *and* their adolescents are asked to complete the Stop-Think Circle. Doing this exercise helps the parents to let go of some of the normal adolescent behaviours that they do not need to challenge and to think about saving their energies for the unacceptable behaviours. It is also the beginnings of new house rules. The process of the exercise means that the parents must communicate with their young people in order to have them complete it.

Session 4

This session takes the group members back to their own adolescence, to remember their own difficulties at that stage of life with behaviour and feelings. The practice task is to take five of the unacceptable behaviours identified in the Stop-Think circle and rate them in order of the behaviours they would like to change, thus helping the parents to decide on their priorities. Parents complete this practice task at home with their adolescents.

Session 5

The focus moves to parenting styles. Three styles are discussed - authoritarian, liberal (laissez-faire) and democratic and the group members consider what their own style of parenting is and how they were parented themselves. The aim is to foster a more democratic approach and an understanding of why this might be more successful. The practice task is to analyse a situation during the week, consider the style of their reaction and how they could have responded more democratically.

Session 6

The theme of the sixth session is communication. In pairs, one person is asked to talk on a subject whilst the other continually interrupts. Then, the pair are asked to play it with one person talking and the other showing no interest at all, for instance looking out of the window and avoiding eye contact. Lastly, the concept of active listening is explained and discussed and the group members practise eye contact and no interruptions. This is a very powerful exercise and it invariably makes a strong impression. The practice task for this session is to choose an appropriate time during the coming week (and what could be 'appropriate' is rehearsed in the group) and actively listen to the young person.

Session 7

The theme is negotiation and the notion of 'best time' to challenge a situation. Examples are explored, such as the futility of challenging a young person who has just come home late and is under the influence of drugs or alcohol. How might group members create a win-win outcome? The practice task is to revisit the five behaviour changes identified in session 4 and to negotiate sanctions and rewards with the adolescent. This reinforces the communication issues which were introduced in the previous session.

Session 8

This session continues the theme of negotiation by considering how boundaries are set, inviting parents to present difficult situations and how the group might respond to them. The significance of timing is reinforced (for example, that adolescents may talk more freely when sat by your side on a car journey or when playing a game). The practice task is to continue to negotiate the rewards and sanctions.

Session 9

This penultimate session explores self-esteem, assertiveness and looking after yourself. The group thinks about what they enjoy, what they feel good about and how they can take time out to recharge their batteries. The importance of having energy to cope with the difficulties is established, and therefore the need to know how to look after energy levels. The practice task is to identify activities that will help group members to look after themselves. They also focus on something that their adolescent is good at and on developing it with lots of praise.

Session 10

The final session is largely an evaluation of the group and its impact. Various resources (reading matter, contacts and organisations) are made available, as well as a certificate of attendance. The group leaders encourage the members to continue contact with each other for support.

The evaluation

South Gloucestershire Youth and Children's Services Department commissioned an evaluation of its groupwork service. This included a stock take of groups past and present, as well as planning for the future. In particular, survey work by the researchers was conducted to highlight the groupwork service's strengths and pinpoint the concerns. The main strengths were seen as the opportunities for co-working and professional development (and the sharing that this entails), and the value of groups for the members. The flexibility of the group content and structure, group planning arrangements and the opportunities for multi-disciplinary work also figured prominently. In terms of action needed, two priority areas emerged. One was the question of publicity for groups (and the appropriateness of referrals) and the other was the need for more consistent and systematic evaluation of the groups. In particular, long-term outcomes of groupwork interventions were not known and there was no specific follow-up with group members after the groups finished. The groupworkers wanted to learn more about what difference, if any, the groups were making.

Of course, service evaluation is unquestionably important for reasons such as accountability, efficiency, planning, development of appropriate programmes and improvement of existing programmes (Alston & Bowles, 2003). What is less conclusive is what methods are the most effective and reliable for which aspects of the evaluation (Grinnell, 1993). If the *delivery* of the service uses groupwork, it seems congruent to incorporate group methods in the *evaluation* of the service (Wheelan, 2005). Yet in the agency in question there was a reliance on individual evaluations (of the 'how was it for you' variety) which probably reflects the broader picture. So, finding out how the groups are working and what difference this is making was typically being focused on the individuals in the group, not on the group as a whole.

Participant observation

Participant observation has an established history as a humanistic research method in the qualitative tradition (Jorgensen, 1989).

> Observational techniques ... can provide new insights by drawing attention to actions and behaviour normally taken for granted by those involved in programme activities and therefore not commented upon in interviews. (Clarke with Dawson, 1999, p.81)

As a method of research it lends itself naturally to groups, though we would argue that its value is considerably enhanced if the participant observer is skilled enough both to participate in groupwork and to observe group process at the same time. Indeed, we might think of adept group members as participant observers, since they actively participate in the group whilst also observing the process.

Ethical considerations are prominent in participant observation, especially concerning whether consent is informed, openly given and can be withdrawn during the process. Especial care must be taken when the participant observation is in a group, in case group pressures have led some reluctant members to acquiesce. Although there may be some rare circumstances which justify the deception of covert participant observation, such as Whyte's (1955) street gangs, in this current study the very fact that the participant was known to be a researcher was important to the process. Although Alston and Bowles (2003) caution that 'subjects will be less likely to disclose sensitive and critical information and they may be inclined to change their behaviour to conform to what is seen as socially desirable', this rests on a largely untested common-sense thesis. As we will see in the following illustration, it is possible that an outsider-becomes-temporary-insider might prompt levels of reflection and disclosure that the group had not previously achieved.

> *Group think* can operate so that individual members feel afraid to voice their true opinions and diversity is lost. Much depends on the skill of the group facilitator. (Alston & Bowles, 2003, p.120)

Some techniques, such as the nominal group, allow ideas to be generated and evaluated by individuals within a group and, by a process of prioritisation, help the group to achieve a consensus. This avoids some of these potential problems of group pressure (Delbecq & Van de Ven, 1971; Potter, Gordon & Hamer, 2004). All three facilitators of the Managing Difficult Behaviour group reported that the group was operating consensually whilst accommodating divergent views and they felt it was robust enough for a whole group method to be used. They saw much potential for reviewing the group from a fresh perspective via the participant observer.

There is a judgement to be made about how much participation there should be. For example, the observer could have participated merely for the 45 minutes of the evaluation slot. If taking part in the whole session, does the observer engage in group rounds? As a groupworker, it is important to negotiate the degree of participation that will be most appropriate for the group; as a researcher, it is a question of which arrangements will yield the most meaningful data (Patton, 1990). Our hypothesis is that these propositions are directly linked and that arrangements that benefit the group process are likely to benefit the research data, too.

Documentary sources of evidence concerning the group's effectiveness came from the groupworkers' own logs, made immediately after each session of the group and the individuals' written evaluations before the group began, mid-way through the group and at the end. These are all primary sources of evidence for the evaluation (Burgess, 1984).

The role of the participant observer

Gold (1969) describes four kinds of role in observation: complete participant, participant-as-observer, observer-as-participant and complete observer. None of these quite fits the bill for our purposes, which led us to develop the notion of 'temporary insider' as a better description of the role in this research, building on McDermott's (2005) notion of insider and outsider perspectives when researching groupwork. This 'dip-in' temporary insider role is, therefore, a different variant of participant observation, which classically involves a longer period. When the temporary insider has a good knowledge of groupwork this can change the role of participant observer into a co-facilitator, but the very temporary nature of this transformation can enable the insider to remain independent. For example, some fifteen minutes into the evaluation one person had been silent, except in response to the first round, and the evaluator made exactly the kind of judgement a groupworker does about whether to ask her to volunteer a view.

The evaluator was also familiar with the task of assisting the members to reflect on themselves *as a group*. The nature of the questions emphasized the group and not just the individual, and they were addressed to the group as a whole as we will see later. A decision has to be made about whether the groupworkers should absent themselves; in this case, the evaluation did not focus directly on the groupworkers and the group was working effectively, so it was decided that they should stay. Having groupworkers present as non-participant observers to the group's evaluation ('temporary outsiders!') has the benefit of their hearing the evaluation directly and it is experienced as a more adult and trusting process than having them leave the room.

Observers, even passive ones, are likely to have some kind of impact on what they are observing. Often this is considered to be a problem (as in the so-called Hawthorne effect, which suggests that people might have a propensity to behave in ways they perceive the researcher to want them to behave), but it can also be a benefit. For example, an unintended consequence of this example of a temporary insider at work was the way that this role actively promoted the development of a *whole group* identity. On a number of occasions, people remarked that 'we haven't really thought about it this way before', but that 'now we think about it', etc. Although the groupworkers themselves could have led a sequence for the group to reflect on itself as a group, in some ways perhaps it is easier for an outsider with a temporary 'visa' to release this.

How the evaluation was established

The groupworkers explained the possible benefits to be derived from evaluating the group and the agency's desire to have its groupwork services evaluated. During the second session they gained group members' informed consents to the attendance of a researcher towards the end of the next session, the third of ten. This verbal consent was given by all group members and it was agreed that the researcher would be present for the whole session (including the pre-group refreshments), with the formal evaluation confined to a given 30-45 minute period towards the end of the session.

How the evaluation was conducted

Having agreed that the evaluator would participate in the whole group, there were decisions about levels of participation. In fact, the observer took an active part in the same elements as the facilitators (in some rounds for example, but not all). The evaluator did not introduce or facilitate any of the segments of the group, apart from the designated one. It is important to note that the evaluation was not a observation of the group from which then to make inferences, the pitfalls of which have been demonstrated by Winstein (1982). Nor was it a systematic, quantitative approach, clocking the pattern, direction and frequency of exchanges between group participants in the style of interaction analysis. In fact the evaluation consisted of a structured conversation with the group, using these questions:

1   How did you get to know about the group?
2   What do you hope the group will do for you?
3   How do you think a group can help (in other words, what is different about the group compared to working with someone individually?)
4   What are you most enjoying about this group?
5   Are there things you'd like to change about the group, or other things you'd like to do?
6   When the group finishes, how will you know that the group has been a success?
7   Would it be OK for me to meet you individually or as couples six months after the group finishes to see what your memories

of the group are then, and whether the group is still having an impact on you?

Each of these questions was asked into the circle of the full group of twelve people (seven women and five men) without being directed towards any particular person. Without discussion, the group chose to use the first question as a round, each person responding in turn. After this, questions were treated as open discussions, generating such discussion that prompts were not needed, merely the occasional request for clarification or elaboration. Permission was asked to use a laptop to make immediate notes, a technique familiar to the participant observer. Sometimes it was difficult to type and process and listen at the same time, but the group responded well to requests to 'just go back and check what you were saying'. The observer knew everyone's name by this stage, which aided the process, though no differentiation between who was saying what was made in the notes. Very soon after the session the observer went over the typed notes to correct and tidy them.

These are the notes from the group's reflections.

Now the group has begun ...

1. **How did you get to know about the group?**
   All members came to the group via some form of contact with social services. For two members attending the group was part of a 'list of things that had to be done'. The police and education welfare service were involved in two other situations.

2. **What do you hope the group will do for you?**
   I'd like a magic wand, but I know there isn't one!; cope with the outbursts; deal with the behaviour as a couple; I need to know how to help him [son]; I want to deal with the situation more calmly; talking will help manage my son's behaviour in a consistent way; I want to get a better understanding; I want better communication and mutual respect; I want to feel more confident as a parent; I want to know what is wrong; I want to learn how to get them [the adolescents] to communicate with me.

3. **How do you think a group can help (what is different about the group compared to working with someone individually?)**
   You're not on your own - you don't feel stupid; you meet with people who are experiencing things that are very similar; I'm glad

that I came - I found out that others have difficulties and in some ways worse off than my situation; the group puts it in perspective; I learn from other people; not feeling alone with your problem; issues are similar and it makes you feel better; able to laugh about it; good to be away from it - the nervous twitch comes back at 8:20pm! [ten minutes before the end of the group]; it's difficult for others [who are not group members] to understand what you're living through; you get acceptance here; family and friends judge you as a bad parent, but here [in the group] they don't; I don't feel judged here; [coming to the group] shows I'm committed; you learn that people have different tolerance levels; people here are dealing with it - at least we care enough to be here; it's a sign of caring [being in the group].

4   **What are you most enjoying about this group?**
Responses were similar to Question 3, plus:
Everybody's company; I feel sorry for people's situations; time away from it [the situation at home]; talking to others; the only time I laugh in the whole week!; a relaxed atmosphere; informative; the group gives me hope; it leads to increased communication; this group is therapy.

5   **Are there things you'd like to change about the group, or other things you'd like to do?**
It's a bit short - I'd like more time [most of the group agree with this]; two hours would be great; it flies by too quick; two sessions a week; perhaps have the first session one and a half hours - I wouldn't have come if I thought it'd be two hours, but then lengthen it as we get used to each other!

6   **When the group finishes, how will you know that the group has been a success?**
We're still keeping in touch as a group; carry on supporting each other; I will have a strategy for how to confidently deal with my son; the group will have given me new ideas; we'll be more of a friend to him [son] by the end of the group; I'll know if I've taken something out of it [but couldn't be specific yet]; to have been able to lower my expectations [of the adolescent's behaviour]; have a growing awareness of how to make it [the relationship and the behaviour] better; have more self-esteem as a parent; have a better idea of whether I am doing it right, as a parent.

7 Would it be OK for me to meet you individually about six months after the group finishes to see what your memories of the group are then, and whether the group is still having an impact on you?

Everyone agreed to this. The researcher will contact people in the autumn, via the groupworkers. Group members can, of course, change their minds in the meantime.

Findings from the evaluation

To what extent had the group become 'a group'? Perhaps we first need to define the characteristics of a group. Although taken from proceedings in 1959 and written in the gendered language of the time, these characteristics are as apt now as they were then and a useful reminder of the timelessness of groups:

(a) close emotional ties among the members
(b) each individual feels that he [*sic*] belongs to the group
(c) each individual feels that he is accepted by the others
(d) the group creates its own structure through which responsibilities are assigned to the various members by common agreement among them
(e) the members of the group have a feeling of loyalty towards the group so that they serve and defend it.

(from: *European Seminar on The General Principles of Social Group Work*, 1959, p.8)

There is evidence in the responses to 'Now the Group Has Begun ...' to support all five elements above. Element (d) was evidenced in the way the group managed itself throughout the session and the sharing of responsibility for the Closing Circle described earlier. The significant aspect of the evaluation was the focus on *the group*. This is in contrast to many evaluations which tend to focus on the *individual* gains. The questions prompted group-oriented responses, peppered with reflections on how the group had affected individuals.

Follow through

The notes from the session were returned to the groupworkers who checked them out with the group members to see if they felt they were accurate. No changes were requested. A follow through visit was made six months later. This particular group did not continue meeting beyond the ten weeks, despite the strong sense of 'groupness', so a call was sent out to all the group members by the workers. Just two people (a couple) came to the follow-up meeting and one person sent her apologies. We discuss this disappointing turn-out later. The couple's responses to the evaluator's post-group interview is recorded below as *Since the group ended ...*

Since the group ended ...
Remembering the group.

Name of the Group: Managing Difficult Behaviour

Date: 6 months since the group ended

Your names: Richard and Mandy

How you were called in the group: *Same*

1   **Thinking back, what were the main reasons you came to the group?**
Both*: To find ways to handle George [our son] when he was in a temper. Learning tips to handle difficult behaviour. Seeing how other people were coping in the same kind of situation - what were their experiences and suggestions were. Looking for different opinions and views.*

2   **Thinking back, what did you hope the group could do for you?**
Both: *We were hoping to learn different techniques.*
Richard*: Being honest I didn't think the group could do anything. I thought, well I'm going to show willing, but it's George who's got the problem, not me. But I went because I wanted to show George that I was prepared to work at it.*
Mandy*: I knew we needed help. I thought the group could help.*

3   **What benefits did you get from the group at the time?**

Richard: *Not feeling alone with the problems. We learned quite a few parenting skills and new ways of handling the situation. Learning to negotiate was really important, though I also found it very infuriating because it takes two to negotiate (i.e. George wouldn't). I also learned that anger begets anger, but I learned to manage it. One of my past bosses said 'if the client's ranting and raving on the phone, say nothing and eventually they'll run out of steam'. George gets fed up if you don't bite. I negotiate at a low level without aggression.*

Mandy: *To see Richard calmer helped me. Being able to manage situations at home in a calmer fashion. It helped me that other parents were going through similar things, sometimes worse things. The homework was good and it was never a problem getting George [our son] to do it. I enjoyed the group meetings - I felt I could open up and express anxieties. We all learned from each other. When you spoke out about your problems you could see other people being helped by hearing about them. I could see others picking up on the 'money drawer' [a technique that Richard and Mandy used with George].*

4   **Have these benefits lasted? If so, how have they been maintained?**

Both: *Yes - for us. For the overall situation no, in fact George is worse. But it may lead to the overall situation changing at some time. We soon realised that they were* parenting *sessions - for the parents, not for the kids. They were about habit forming - getting into different ways of doing things.*

Since the group Richard and Mandy no longer disagree with one another. *We're working together more now. He gets the same from both of us. If we do have a difference we sort it out away from George.*

5   **If the benefits didn't last what might have helped keep them going?**

Both: *We're going to carry on with the plan we've got. George will learn.*

6   **With hindsight, what other things, if any, could the group have done that would have improved it?**

Both: *If it could have gone a bit longer. We would have liked even more open discussion and longer sessions. Not necessarily every time, but maybe another hour on this particular night, a half-hour on that night, if it was going well. We understand the groupworkers have a life, too, but sometimes it just felt too short.*

Richard: *I was never looking at my watch, in fact I'd look at my watch and think, have we only got fifteen minutes left.*

Both: *Follow-up sessions every two months would be good; after two months, then four, then six. Get feedback from other group members. It'd be better if it was a follow-up just for us [the members of that particular group] but we could understand if, because of people's time, we had to meet up with other groups, too. We'd want a worker there, to structure it.*

7 If the group was starting again would you recommend it?
Both: *Yes.*

Although it'd be good to have longer sessions and to go on for longer than just ten weeks, we can see how people might be put off if they thought they were committing to a longer period.

8 On a scale of 1 - 10 (1= not at all; 10 = completely) how successful was the group for you?
Mandy: *7/10*
Richard: *8/10*

Both felt it was an excellent group and Richard thought he probably scored even higher than Mandy because he had lower expectations of the group than Mandy.

9 In what ways did the groupworkers help you?
Both: *They were brilliant - calm, relaxed and relaxing. There was really good input - useful information. They were very flexible, no dictating. They would assess the mood of the group and go with that. They had an agenda, but they could be flexible with it. And then they'd always bring us back on track. They sympathised with us, they understood. Their professionalism was superb. They'd listen and come out with constructive ideas. They weren't condescending and everything sounded fresh, not like they'd done it lots of times before. You felt you had some form of support. Yes, it was their professionalism. The only thing we'd want different was to be able to have extended some of the sessions and meet up regularly after the group finished.*

Reflections on the follow up

What is most striking about this follow up is the fact that only three of the twelve members of the group responded to the request for contact. It is impossible to know what this might indicate and there are many possible explanations, from the group being so successful that participants did not want to be reminded of previous less happy times, to the group having so little medium-term impact that the group members felt embarrassed or angry about the prospect of turning out again. Like silence in a group, absence from the recall is difficult to interpret. The fact that the group members did not continue to meet after the ten week sessions undoubtedly reduced the chances of a response six months later. Yet the groupworkers felt this was a group that had gelled very well and they were surprised that members had gone their separate ways. We considered making a further call, but time and distance (between researcher and group members) made this problematic. Also, it is difficult to judge how appropriate it is to pursue participants, much the same as the dilemma groupworkers have about group members who do not show; except that any permission to pursue felt very tenuous six months after the group members had given their goodbyes.

The other curious finding was the fact that, though Mandy and Richard both rated the group highly, they felt that their son's behaviour was on balance worse than at the time of the group! What had transformed their lives (the word they themselves used) was their response to their son's behaviour, which they attributed entirely to the group. Although it is the testimony of only two people, it is nevertheless a strong message about the complexity of outcome-based evaluations. If we measure the group's impact against the son's behaviour it failed; if measured against how the parents are managing themselves in relation to that behaviour, it has been an outstanding success. Mandy and Richard felt motivated to turn out these six months later to explain this; they were not seeking 'new advice' or continuing work and felt able to continue to use the skills and confidence that they had developed in the group. They had been looking forward to renewing contact with the group members and expressed considerable surprise and regret that no others were there.

Good practice in participant observation in groups

Given the suggestion that 'practitioners of participant observation have resisted formulating definitive procedures and techniques' (Jorgensen, 1989. p.8), the following practice principles are given with some caution. The significance of any one guideline is, of course, likely to differ from one group to another and one participant observation to another.

- clear communication with the group about the rationale and purpose of the observation
- clear understanding of the difference between the observer and the groupworkers
- discussion on when during the group's life the observation is best made
- informed consent from all group members, so it is they who invite the observer
- consideration of the observer's role and how much to be involved in group processes
- preparation around how the evaluation will fit with the session and contingencies if the evaluation leads to difficult or strong emotions
- active use made of the observer's status as a temporary insider
- agreement with the group about how observations will be recorded and corroborated
- agreement with the group about follow up and how information will be used.

We have considered the notion of participant observer as temporary insider and the possible value of this idea in practice. We need more systematic experience on which to build the evidence base (Preston-Shoot, 2004; Trevithick, 2005). However, these experiences suggest that a temporary insider can balance independence from the group with the opportunity to influence group processes positively, in order to help groups to evaluate themselves. There is some evidence to suggest that the role of temporary insider can be used as a positive force to encourage the development of a *group* identity.

References

Alston, M. & Bowles, W. (2003) *Research for Social Workers: An introduction to methods.* London: Routledge

Burgess, R.G. (1984) *In the Field: An introduction to field research.* London: George Allen and Unwin

Clarke, A. with Dawson, R. (1999) *Evaluation Research.* London: Sage

Delbecq, A.L. and Van de Ven, A.H. (1971) A group process model for problem identification and program planning. *Journal of Applied Behavioural Science,* 7, 4, 466-492

Doel, M. (2006) *Using Groupwork.* London: Routledge/Community Care

Gold, R.L. (1969) *Issues in Participant Observation,* Reading: Addison-Wesley

Grinnell, R.M. (Ed.) (1993) *Social Work Research and Evaluation.* [3rd ed] Itasca, Ill: Peacock

Jorgensen, D.L. (1989) *Participant Observation: A methodology for human studies.* Newbury Park, PA: Sage

Malekoff, A. (2004) *Group Work with Adolescents: Principles and practice.* (2nd ed.] New York: Guilford Press

McDermott, F. (2005) Researching groupwork: Outsider and insider perspectives. *Groupwork,* 15, 1, 90-108

Patton, M.Q. (1990) *Qualitative Evaluation and Research Methods.* [2nd ed.] Newbury Park, CA: Sage

Potter, M., Gordon, S., & Hamer, P. (2004) The nominal group technique: A useful consensus methodology. *NZ Journal of Physiotherapy,* 32, 3, 126-30

Preston-Shoot, M. (2004) Evidence: the final frontier? Star Trek, groupwork and the mission of change. *Groupwork,* 14, 3, 18-40

Trevithick, P. (2005) The knowledge base of groupwork and its importance within social work. *Groupwork,* 15, 2, 80-107

Wheelan, S. A. (2005) *The Handbook of Group Research and Practice.* Thousand Oaks, CA: Sage

Whyte, W.F. (1955) *Street Corner Society.* Chicago: Chicago University Press

Winstein, R.M. (1982) The mental hospital from the patient's point of view. in Walter R. Gove [Ed.] *Deviance and Mental Illness.* Thousand Oaks, CA: Sage

7
Dancing towards wholeness:
The impact of conflict on patterns
of interpersonal coordination
in a small treatment group

William Pelech and Robert Basso

Summary

This paper examines how patterns of interpersonal coordination are influenced by interpersonal conflict in treatment groups. Interpersonal coordination is operationalized as a means of examining changing patterns of nonverbal behaviour in a social treatment group. Interpersonal coordination is defined as comprising two behavioural elements, behavioural congruence and interpersonal synchrony. Cluster analysis is creatively utilized to graphically depict patterns of interpersonal coordination. Cluster plots from two treatment sessions are presented to demonstrate the value of cluster analysis in portraying changing patterns of interpersonal coordination over time. Included in the discussion are the implications of this new approach for group work research.

Introduction

> Within the intricate web of the community associations form, dissolve, combine and separate in a complicated and ever changing pattern. (Grace Coyle, 1930, p. 38)

It has been over seventy years since Grace Coyle described the dynamic nature of interpersonal bonds within groups. The tools available at that time were limited to the use of keen observational skills. However, today advances in technology and statistical methods offer new approaches and tools, some which may serve to re-examine some of our beliefs about the nature of group development. One such new approach is the application of cluster analysis to the study of patterns of nonverbal behaviour in small groups.

Conflict, like interpersonal bonds, has also been a topic of many years of study and discourse in the annals of group work literature. Hartford (1972) conceptualized interpersonal bonds as being affected by the presence of conflict. As Hartford noted:

Over time there may be changes or fluctuations in the degree of cohesion of the group. As the group forms, it is expected that the cohesion will increase, but as the group encounters conflicts and readjustments, the cohesion may decrease. (Hartford , 1972, pp. 250-251)

With new tools to assist with the study of groups, how does conflict influence the development and preservation of interpersonal bonds in a treatment group?

Theoretical rationale

Bernieri and Rosenthal (1991) delineated two aspects of interpersonal coordination: behavioural congruence and interactional synchrony. Both of these aspects represent the formation of interpersonal bonds or couplings through the entrainment of group members' behaviour on two closely interrelated dimensions. Behavioural congruence relates to how members demonstrate similar (e.g., matching or mirrored postures) nonverbal behaviour over time. Interactional synchrony involves a temporal dimension and measures the extent to which members are moving together in the same cycles or rhythms.

Consonant with our understanding of group cohesion, behavioural congruence appears to indicate the relative togetherness among interactants (e.g., Charny, 1966; Kendon, 1970; LaFrance, 1979, 1985; Scheflen, 1964). According to Scheflen (1964), congruent postures indicate the nature of member interpersonal relationships or associations. Scheflen (1964) theorized that postural congruence was a measure of the togetherness or similarity of two people's internal states, and thus in a group, reflects a shared view by group members. A lack of togetherness may be depicted by a lack of behavioural congruence. Similarly, LaFrance (1979) later concluded in reference to dyads and groups:

Postural mirroring may be uniquely helpful in understanding the ongoing formation, change and dissolution of these social units.... an observer might similarly be able to gauge the level of cohesion between and among members of an encounter by noting the amount of mirroring displayed. (LaFrance, 1979, p. 292)

The ability to establish interactional synchrony represents an innate human capacity and one of the earliest forms of human communication. Interactional synchrony appears to serve two important functions relevant to effective group treatment. First, it serves the basic survival needs of bonding, safety, and comfort (Condon, 1980; Condon & Sander, 1974). Second, it appears to regulate interpersonal interaction. Many of the studies concerning interactional synchrony have examined infant/mother interaction (e.g., Als, Tronick, & Brazelton, 1979; Bullowa, 1975; Condon & Ogston, 1971; Kempton, 1980; Stern, 1971; Stern, 1985; Tronick, Als, & Brazelton, 1977).

So, it would seem that interpersonal coordination might offer a new way to empirically examine the dynamic patterns of interpersonal bonds in small groups. The next section describes a methodology that attempts to extend this construct of interpersonal coordination from dyads to a small treatment group.

Method

The setting of this research project was a Canadian psychiatric hospital in Ontario Canada. The group studied was composed of eight male clients who had been admitted to the Hospital. Each of the clients participating in the group session had been previously diagnosed as experiencing clinical depression and was taking various types of anti-depressant medication.

Argyle (1988), in his summary of the literature, described four main signals indicative of interpersonal attraction: proximity (including forward lean if seated), gaze or mutual gaze, and open arm and leg positions. Thus, four classes of nonverbal behaviour were measured over each of 12 one-hour group treatment sessions: lean, gaze, arm position, and leg position. Behaviour for each class was then organized on a continuum to create measures of relative engagement (forward lean, gaze towards speaker) and accessibility (openness of legs and arms). These rating scales were pre-tested with several taped sessions to gauge their ability to capture the major types of nonverbal positions.

Analysis

Traditionally used for such large-scale projects as and epidemiological studies, cluster analysis has not heretofore been utilized for the study of patterns of nonverbal behaviour in small groups. A central component of one approach to cluster analysis is the calculation of a dissimilarity matrix. Similar to a distance chart on a road map, a dissimilarity matrix lists the relative distance or dissimilarity of each observation from each other point. The dissimilarity matrix was used to produce graphical displays.

For analysis purposes, each session was broken up into approximately six 10-minute sections, allowing for analysis of the impact of critical events upon interpersonal coordination in the group. To produce a graphic display, not unlike a sociogram, thresholds were needed to depict strong (depicted by solid lines), moderate (depicted by dashed lines), and weak (depicted by dotted lines) as well as little or no relationship between member behaviour. Since there were no previous studies to draw guidance for such thresholds, it was decided that quartiles of each section's distances would be used for creating thresholds. The reliability of behavioural ratings exceeded the .80 standard for reliability estimates (r=.83).

Results

To demonstrate the impact of group development over time, examples of the impact of conflict are offered at the beginning (i.e., first session), and end (i.e., tenth session) of the group. For each session, a descriptive summary of critical events and interactions occurring during portions of the session will be presented. Cluster analysis plots depicting both behavioural congruence and interactional synchrony are presented for each of these sessions. In the plots that follow, each member is identified by an acronym (eg., Ry, Rb, Jn, Sc, Dn, Ty, Pl, & St)while the workers are designated as 'W1' and 'W2.'

Beginning with the first session, Rb, Ry, and Jn were actively engaged in the discussion with W1 concerning the issues of self-esteem and their need for validation. As the group approached the middle of the session, issues of anger and self-assertion emerged in the group. At this point, Dn became the focal point of discussion. Dn shared how he had been victimised by life and depression. As he continued to share his victimised position, several members, especially Pl and Sc, found Dn's continual victim stance to be increasingly intolerable. As the session passed the 40-minute mark, Pl joined in the confrontation with Dn.

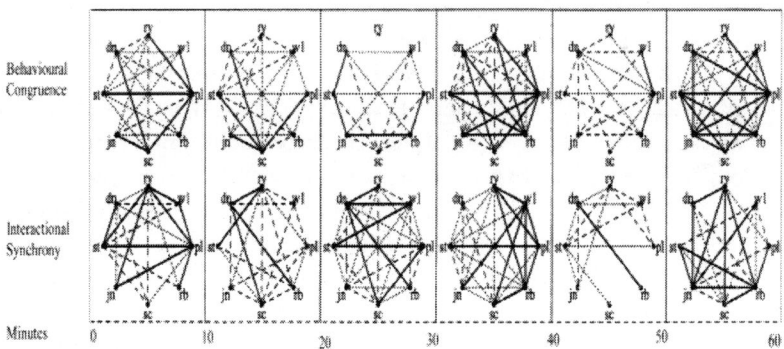

Figure 1
Session One: Cluster Analysis of Interpersonal Coordination (Ten Minute Segments)

Cluster analysis (see Figure 1) reflected the impact of escalating tension with a reduction of interpersonal couplings over this period. When the focus shifted to Dn (fourth segment), a dramatic change occurred with many strong relationships arising between group

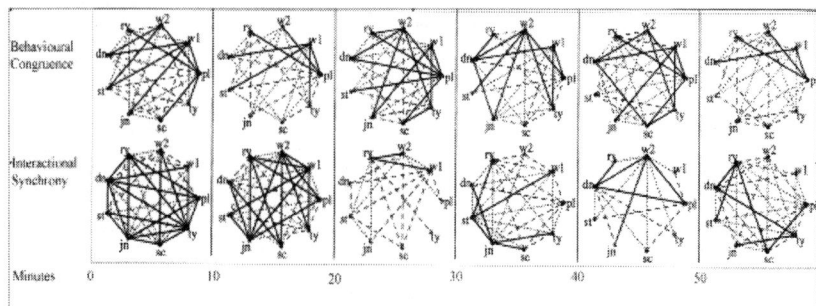

Figure 2
Session Ten: Cluster Analysis of Interpersonal Coordination (Ten Minute
Segments)

members. In reference to behavioural congruence, perhaps indicative
of their mutual engagement, Dn was linked with Sc and Rb, while Sc
was linked with Pl and Dn. Here also, Jn, St, and Ry were all strongly
linked with Pl and Rb. As we move from the fourth to the fifth segment,
coinciding with the long 'tragic' soliloquy by Dn, the synchronous
relationships again shifted dramatically. This segment illustrates the
impact of the angry cathartic assault by Sc and Pl upon Dn. Suddenly,
many of the strong relationships present in segment four dissolved,
leaving only relationships between Pl, Rb, and W1.

Conflict emerged early in Session Ten. After Dn reasserted his
victim position in his relationships with others, Ty asked if any member
present had a violin to accompany Dn's tale of woe. After Dn responded
by criticizing Ty's insensitivity, Ty more vociferously challenged Dn to
express his anger. As the group continued into the middle portion of
the session, Ty attempted to acknowledge Dn's need for validation. Dn
rejected the affirmation, and resentfully stated that he did not need
validation from the group. Sc then intervened in support of Ty, and
challenged Dn and his need to escape the truth. As Dn and Sc begin to
exchange heated words, W1 intervened to offer a summary statement
that affirmed how others were frustrated with Dn. This again triggered
a defensive response from Dn that culminated in a confrontation with
Pl over the inconsistencies in Dn's position and statements. Jn then
intervened to offer a different perspective that affirmed Dn's efforts and
work in the group. Dn responded with appreciation of Jn's kind words.

In terms of cluster analysis (see Figure 2), the first plot offered some
important behavioural couplings. For example, Pl coupled with W1, Ry,
Ty, and Sc, each of whom confronted Dn during the session. Perhaps

indicative of an unprecedented resonance created by Dn's interactions, a densely coupled synchronous structure now emerged over time. Rather than decoupling as they had in earlier sessions, members increased their synchronous couplings in response to Dn's disclosures.

However, while they were able to remain behaviourally engaged, many of the synchronous couplings, perhaps indicative of a lack of empathy, eroded as the group passed the mid-point of the session. In the fourth plot, a most significant shift coincided with Jn's intervention in support of Dn. Differences between the two plots demonstrated some interesting artifacts of the nature of behavioural and synchronous couplings. Note how Dn coupled with or engaged with Ry, Jn, and the workers in the behavioural plot, and yet engaged in synchronous couplings with Jn; the only member who had provided him emotional support.

Discussion

The use of cluster analysis in the study of interpersonal coordination offers several implications and opportunities in the field of small group research. The use of cluster analysis has introduced a new tool for studying the development of interpersonal bonds in small groups. It also provides another way of confirming a vast body of anecdotal evidence, practice wisdom and theoretical concepts present within the field of group work. It provides a clear and compelling graphical representation of the life of a group and its changing structural relationships; producing plots that are easy to interpret and resemble sociometric instruments commonly used by group workers.

Some of the results also offer some very tentative insights into the impact of conflict upon interpersonal bonds. The plots presented may have provided an example of how a group can become what Bion (1970) termed as a 'container' for therapeutic work. While most if not all interpersonal bonds were disrupted during turbulent periods in the early sessions, more behavioural couplings survived later in the tenth session, during what was arguably the most intense conflict experienced during the life of this group. It seemed that at this point the group had developed sufficient bonds to hold the conflict and to maintain mutual engagement through congruent postures. However, engagement does not necessarily mean agreement or an empathetic interpersonal stance.

The implications of this inquiry for group work practice further emphasize the importance of nonverbal behaviour and communication in group settings. As suggested by Middleman and Goldberg-Wood (1990), by scanning patterns of nonverbal behaviour workers may gain insights into the dynamic patterns of engagement, affective responses and interpersonal alliances in a group.

In conclusion, this inquiry has pioneered new approaches to studying treatment groups and has taken group work research into a new realm of discovery. It has extended our understanding of interpersonal coordination from individual and dyadic relationships to group settings. As an exploratory inquiry it has also highlighted the need for further exploration of some fundamental questions and issues.

References

Argyle, M. (1988). *Bodily Communication*. London: Methuen & Co.

Als, H., Tronick, E., & Brazelton, T. (1979). Analysis of face-to-face interaction in infant-adult dyads. In M. Lamb, S. Suomi, & G. Stephenson (Eds.), *Social Interaction Analysis* (pp. 33-76). Madison: University of Wisconsin.

Bernieri, F. & Rosenthal, R. (1991). Interpersonal coordination: Behavior matching and interactional synchrony. In R. Feldman & B. Rime (Eds.), *Fundamentals of Nonverbal Behavior* (401-432). Cambridge: Cambridge University Press.

Bion, W. (1970). *Experiences in Groups and Other Papers*. New York: Basic Books.

Bullowa, M. (1975). When infant and adult communicate, how do they synchronize their behaviors? In A. Kendon, R. Harris, & M. Key (Eds.), *Organization of Behavior in FaceTo-Face Interaction* (pp. 95-125). Paris: Mouton.

Charny, E. (1966). Psychosomatic manifestations of rapport in psychotherapy. *Psychosomatic Medicine*, 28, 305-315.

Condon, W. (1980). The relation of interactional synchrony to cognitive and emotional processes. In M. Key (Ed.), *The Relationship of Verbal and Nonverbal Communication* (pp. 49-65). New York: Mouton.

Condon, W. & Ogston, W. (1971). Speech and body motion synchrony of the speaker-hearer. In D. Horton & J. Jenkins (Eds.), *Perception of Language* (pp. 150-173). Columbus, OH: Charles Merrill.

Condon, W., & Sander, L. (1974). Synchrony demonstrated between movements of the neonate and adult speech. *Child Development*, 45, 456-462.

Coyle, G. (1930). *Social Processes in Organized Groups*. New York: Richard R. Smith.

Everitt, B. (1974). *Cluster Analysis*. London: Heinemann Educational Books.

Hartford, M. (1972). *Groups in Social Work*. New York: Columbia University Press.

Kempton, W. (1980). The rhythmic basis of interactional micro-synchrony. In M. Key (Ed.), *The Relationship of Verbal and Nonverbal Communication* (pp. 67-75). New York: Mouton.

Kendon, A. (1970). Movement coordination in social interaction. *Acta Psychologica*, 32, 100-125.

LaFrance, M. (1979). Nonverbal synchrony and rapport: Analysis by the cross-lagged panel technique. *Social Psychology Quarterly*, 42, 66-70.

LaFrance, M. (1985). Postural mirroring and intergroup relation. *Personality and Social Psychology Bulletin*, 11, 207-217.

Middleman, R., & Goldberg Wood, G. (1990). *Skills for Direct Practice in Social Work*. New York: Columbia University Press.

Scheflen, A. (1964). The significance of posture in communication systems. *Psychiatry*, 27, 316-331.

Stern, D. (1971). A micro-analysis of mother-infant interaction. *Journal of the Academy of Child Psychiatry*, 10, 501-517.

Stern, D. (1985). *Interpersonal Underworld of the Infant*. New York: Basic Books.

Tronick, D., Als, H., & Brazelton, T. (1977). Mutuality in mother-infant interaction. *Journal of Communication*, 27, 47-79.

8

Using the research process to develop group services for older persons with a hearing disability

Timothy B. Kelly, Debbie Tolson, Tracy Day Smith, and Gillian McColgan

Abstract

This paper briefly describes the results of a mixed-methods study that used key informant interviews, surveys, and focus groups to explore what older people think they need to successfully adjust to life with a hearing aid. The older, hearing-impaired people in this study had much to tell group workers about how to facilitate and orchestrate groups designed to help them successfully adjust to life with a hearing aid. Older people were hungry for knowledge and information as well as support and mutual aid. This paper also reports on the use of focus groups in the research process and how mutual aid flourished within the research project. Implications for research and practice are drawn.

Introduction

The ageing of the population in industrialised countries is a well documented phenomenon, and as populations continue to age, health and social care providers will be increasingly required to address the age-related problems that older people face (Timonen, 2008). The potential burden placed on the health and social care sector by this ageing population necessitates finding appropriate, effective, and cost-effective services that will support people as they age.

One of the common age-related physical impairments is age-related hearing loss. In a 1989 study cited by the PHIS report (www.phis.org. uk), 26% of UK adults reported difficulty hearing what was said in moderate noise. Hearing impairment increases with age. Other studies not specific to the UK have found prevalence rates between 40% and 62% (Huang & Tang, 2010; Worrall, Hickson, Barnett & Yiu, 1998). Despite high rates of hearing impairment in older adults, relatively few older persons with a hearing impairment own a hearing aid, and less than half of those who are fitted for hearing aids in the UK still use them eight to 16 years later (Gianopoulous, Stephens & Davis, 2002).

The ability to communicate is an important component of healthy ageing and influences perceptions of the quality of an individual's life. Communication, for example, is required to participate in such things as activities of living, establishing and maintaining friendships, receiving quality care, maintaining social networks, facilitation of adaptation to change, involvement in decision making, and relieving loneliness, depression, and anxiety (Worrall & Hickson, 2003). A hearing impairment can create a functional limitation that impinges on many important areas of life and potentially create other psychological, social, and health problems.

As hearing and communication are so important, and a significant percentage of an ageing population is likely to develop a hearing disability, health care professionals must develop beneficial and cost-effective treatment and intervention strategies that are acceptable to service users. The rejection rate of hearing aids by older people who are fitted with them is high (Gianopoulous, Stephens & Davis, 2002), therefore it becomes even more important to find interventions that are beneficial to individuals, and cost effective for the health service. As such, the aim of this study was to explore what older people needed that would enable them to adjust to and get maximum benefit from wearing a hearing aid. The second aim was to develop a group rehabilitation programme based on older people's views, and ascertain the proposed programmes' acceptability to older service users.

Literature review

The development of audiology following the second world war was rehabilitative in the broadest sense - encompassing testing and fitting of devices, counselling, education, and occupational therapy (Northern & Beyer, 1999; Ross, 1997). Since that time there has been a trend towards a more technical and medical approach. This shift is understandable as the technology, both in assessment and medical devices, became increasingly sophisticated and promising. In the United Kingdom the move towards the technical was further heightened as the demand for hearing aids outstripped the personnel resources. The National Health Service (NHS) developed an "over the counter" approach to supplying hearing aids (Brooks & Johnson, 1981). In essence, this is an individualistic medical model approach. However, there has been a growing consensus and body of evidence suggesting that the provision of technology alone does not meet the needs of older persons (e.g., Abrahamson, 2000; Abrams, Hnath-Chisolm, Guerreiro & Ritterman, 1992; Binzer, 2002; Brooks & Johnson, 1981; Gatehouse, 2003; Hickson & Worrall, 2003; Northern & Beyer, 1999; Ross, 1997). Thankfully, a body of literature is developing that describes various rehabilitation programmes consisting of some form of counselling and/or education (see, e.g., Abrahamson, 2000 & 1991; Abrams, Hnath-Chisolm, Guerreiro, Ritterman, 1992; Alberti, Pichora-Fuller, Corbin & Riko., 1984; Benyon, Thorton & Poole, 1997; Binnie, 1977; Bizner, 2002; Brickly, Cleaver & Bailey, 1996; Cunningham, 1996; DiSarno, 1997; Hawkins, 2005; Hickson, Worrall, Yiu & Barnett, 1996; Kricos, Holmes & Doyle, 1992; Laplante-Levesque, Hickson & Worrall, 2010; Lesner, 1992; Northern & Beyer, 1999; Ross, 1997; Rubinstein & Boothroyd, 1987; Taylor & Jurma, 1999; Tolson, 1997; Ward & Gowers, 1981). However, there is still some resistance by professionals to provide more counselling and education to older people who need hearing aids. Reasons for this resistance that are most frequently cited are concerns about cost and time (Kricos, 1997). For example, Hickson, Timm, and Worrall (1999) suggest that the cost of rehabilitation must be justified, as it is expensive.

Despite the frequent calls for rehabilitation services to encompass more than the technological remediation of the hearing loss and the well documented rejection of hearing aids by older hearing-impaired adults, there is surprisingly little literature that evaluates counselling and educationally-based aural rehabilitation programmes. Studies to date, such as those described above, have suggested mixed results, and most of the research has been fraught with methodological problems. One consistency in the research, however, is the improvement in the outcome measures for all the studies, albeit not consistently at a significant level. Several explanations for this are possible. First, most studies have had very small participant numbers. Results from small-scale studies can lack statistical power, which in turn can prevent real changes from being detected because statistical significance is not reached. However, the failure to reach statistical significance in quantitative results can be the result of a small sample size rather than the result of an ineffective intervention. The interventions in the studies were modest (from one to five sessions) and in all likelihood had limited effect size. Second, some studies (e.g., Abrams et al., 2002) used outcome measure that were not hearing specific or that were not sensitive enough to detect changes in the brief training provided (e.g., Kricos, Holmes, & Doyle, 1992). Third, most of the studies included interventions that were highly didactic and programmed focusing on the remediation of the hearing impairment. Having highly scripted and consistent interventions can improve the internal validity of studies, but it may also interfere with the effectiveness of an intervention, because such controlled interventions may not meet the needs of group or class members. In order for groups to be most effective, they must meet the unique needs of each group, and Hogan (2001) suggests the use of a psychosocial problem-solving approach, which focuses on participants' definitions, exploration, and resolution of their respective communication difficulties. Therefore, by focusing on the hearing impairment rather than the functional limitations experienced by individual subjects with a hearing impairment, the interventions may not have addressed the needs and problems in living that the subjects were actually experiencing, which could reduce the potential effectiveness of the group. Finally, only one of the studies reviewed to date used an involving methodology (Hickson et al., 1996), but this study designed a communication programme for older people in general and not designed specifically for rehabilitation. Given the inconsistent findings and lack of user involvement, the researchers wished to involve older service users in developing a group-based audiological rehabilitation programme that can meet the needs of older adults.

Methods

A mixed-methods research design was employed in the study. This included:

- Semi-structured interviews with nine key professionals from six different organisations across Scotland who provide services to older people with hearing impairments.
- Random survey of two groups of older people; the instruments used for the study (a questionnaire and focus groups) were designed to explore what would make it easier for older people to adjust to life with hearing loss and the need to use a hearing aid. The questionnaire was based on issues found in the literature review and interviews with key informants. The survey was completed by older people who were:
  - o On waiting lists for a hearing aid (n=85)
  - o Hearing aid users (n=155)
- Focus groups with older audiology patients (n=31, 14 men and 17 women aged 60-87 years old) to explore and deepen the understanding of the survey results. Initially the nominal group technique was used to this end, but as will be explained later this approach was quickly abandoned.
- Focus groups with older audiology patients (n=26, 16 men and 10 women aged 57-86 years old) to review and provide feedback on a group rehabilitation programme developed from the results of the survey and first round of focus groups.

Quantitative data were analysed using SPSS. Qualitative data were analysed using thematic content analysis and was facilitated by the use of N-Vivo.

Results

Here are the key findings of the study along with results that are particularly interesting from a groupwork perspective. First, the professionals who participated in the semi-structured interviews agreed that more information and follow-up support is required as part of the audiology services for older people to address (1) how to access and get services; (2) communication; (3) psychological issues; (3) mechanics of hearing aid use; (4) advice for dealing with practical problems; (5) education; and (6) support.

Survey results with hearing-impaired older adults indicate that older people want information and support both before and after receiving a hearing aid. For example, amongst the respondents who use hearing aid, only 56% feel confident about using their hearing aids or in their ability to use the controls on the aid. The key finding related to this component of the study is clearly that information and support are needed and wanted by older people. Participants in the first round of focus groups reiterated that the primary need *prior to* hearing aid fitting is preparatory information and focused on processes and realistic expectations. Needs *after* fitting were identified primarily as (1) information on equipment operation and (2) tips on good communication. Additionally, support was required for adjusting to life with a hearing aid. Finally, many participants had concerns for the cosmetics of hearing aids.

Based on the results of the survey and initial focus groups, a proposed programme was developed. In the proposed programme, people would receive an information booklet when the decision was made that they needed an aid, and an ear mould would be taken at that time. After receiving their hearing aid, they would be invited to attend a group programme consisting of three to four sessions in which additional information and support would be provided. The purpose of the proposed group would be to help older people to use their hearing aids and to adjust to wearing them in order to get the most benefit from them.

In order for groups to be most effective, they must meet the unique needs of each group, and therefore, a strict curriculum-based programme was not recommended. However, based on the research literature and the results from this study, there are likely informational and support needs that would be important to include in a group-rehabilitation programme. As such, a flexible structure and the development and availability of written resources to supplement group discussions would assist with meeting the needs of older people in this kind of group setting.

The proposed structure would include a first session to explain the purpose of the group, move to a discussion of participants' personal experience with their hearing aids, and then identify and list the difficulties currently experienced, a problem-identification process that would serve as the basis for future sessions. As such, subsequent sessions would address the problems identified in the first session as well as any others that might surface. In addition, if desired by participants a brief educational component would be planned for each session to include (1) the mechanics of hearing, (2) hearing loss, (3) hearing aids, (4) hearing tests, (5) maintenance and care of hearing aids, (6) environmental aids, (7) communication skills, and (8) assertiveness. Written materials would be also prepared to cover likely topics of concern such as those identified by the questionnaire used in this study.

In the focus groups conducted to review the proposed rehabilitation programme, participants liked the concept of an *information booklet*. There was also overwhelming support for the idea of group-support services, and it was suggested that after being fitted with a hearing aid, all people should be referred to such a group. A few changes were suggested to the group programme presented for review, but overall, participants expressed the wish that they had had the opportunity to participate in such a service.

Groupwork lessons from the research process

The researchers learned several important lessons in the research process that have important implications for group workers and/or researchers. These lessons include (1) factoring in mutual aid to research designs, (2) including service users in programme design, and (3) the place of curriculum-driven groups in this area of service.

The place of mutual aid in research design

The first lesson is surprisingly unexpected - namely that mutual aid began to develop in the focus groups. Being a group worker it should not have been surprising that mutual aid could develop in what was a single-session group in which all participants shared a common problem and had common needs (Steinberg, 2004). The original research protocol for the focus groups was the *Nominal Group Technique*, a decision-making method for use by groups of all sizes that want to make decision quickly but also want everyone's opinions taken into account (Delbecq & Van de Ven, 1971). The plan was to introduce a question and to ask participants to respond in a notebook after which each group member would list his/her answers and rank them in order of importance. We thought this format would minimise barriers for people with hearing disability. However, from the very first session this very controlled and structured approach was quickly abandoned after introducing the first question, which was as follows:

> The survey shows that people want information and support both before and after receiving a hearing aid. What do you think is most important for people to learn about BEFORE they get their hearing aid?

In response to this question participants immediately began to discuss what they thought they needed to know, as well as the difficulties they had experienced as a result of not being informed. In fact, there was a huge burst of energy in responding to this question, and the discussions seemed cathartic as the "all in the same boat" phenomenon seemed to kick in.

As researchers and group workers we had a bit of a dilemma: Do we throw the research protocol out the window, or do we let the mutual aid develop? In the heat of the moment we decided that the information we needed to answer the research questions was being provided – albeit in a less structured way – and that the focus group was also providing a service of sorts and so went along with the process. This adjusted approach was then followed in the subsequent focus groups, in each of which examples of mutual-aid dynamics (Shulman, 1999; Steinberg, 2004) surfaced. This included:

- Sharing data – a great deal of information and resources were exchanged.
- Dialectical process – participants were quick to express differing opinions, especially around issues of cosmetic concerns, and new ideas emerged from these discussion.
- Mutual support – emotional support was provided (e.g., feeling isolated from family and friends).
- Individual problem solving – people shared current problems they were having and other participants gave assistance (e.g., dealing with wind noise, how to ask people to speak up or face you when speaking).
- Rehearsal – In several of the sessions more experienced hearing aid users showed participants how to use a loop system and

communication using a loop system was practiced during the data collection discussions.

This experience left us with some questions:

- Are researchers cognisant of the potential for mutual aid to develop when designing studies?
- What are the implications if such a possibility is not factored into research design?

The development of mutual aid was a benefit for the participants in the focus groups. Yet when the study was approved by the University's and National Health Service's Research Ethics Committees, there was no mention of this benefit for participants. Rather, the research ethics applications outlined potential risks to participants and how we as researchers would mitigate against those risks. Granted, it would be unethical to suggest benefits if they are unlikely, but had we identified the potential benefit of mutual aid, recruitment of participants might have been facilitated. The participant information sheet indicated that no personal benefit was likely, but more people may have participated if the potential for personal support through mutual aid was highlighted. Perhaps researchers who use focus groups as a data-collection method should factor the potential of mutual aid into their participant information sheets. Given that the potential for mutual aid had not been identified as a component of the study, it could be argued that we should have remained true to the research protocol as originally designed. However, the needs of the participants were so palpable and their emergent mutual aid so spontaneous and powerful that to rigidly adhere to research protocol felt like a potential breach of a duty of care. As a result, the research protocol was adapted to accommodate this powerful need and then replicated in subsequent focus groups. On hindsight, this approach should have been built into the research design from the beginning. However, the experience was an important research finding in and of itself – a finding that strongly supports the development of a group service for this population.

Involving service users in the design of services

There is a growing international movement to involve service users in the design and development of services (Kelly et al., 2006; Tolson et al., 2007), and this study highlights the importance of this in a group format. For example, key informants listed much of what older people said they wanted in a rehabilitation programme; however, it was not a complete match with what was anticipated. When the proposed programme was developed from service-user feedback and shown to all hearing therapists in Scotland, they thought that it was too much information. Finally, when this was raised in the final round of focus groups, service users were unanimous in saying that the hearing therapists were wrong. Perhaps the "strength in numbers" dynamic of mutual aid kicked in during the focus groups, allowing them to disagree with the experts. In contrast to what had been indicated by the hearing therapists, participants wanted as much information as possible and wanted to be involved in designing the format of that information.

Professionals also had some reservations about referring people to a group service; yet, focus group participants felt that all audiology patients should be referred to a group after receiving a hearing aid as a part of standard service. They understood that some people may not want to attend a group but felt that if the group was designed and presented in a way that would *CLEARLY* meet their needs, people would attend. (Approximately 50% of the survey respondents indicated that they would attend a group).

Balance between curriculum driven and needs driven group

The research participants also had something to say regarding the current debate about curriculum-driven groupwork. They indicated that they were not so interested in a "class" where each session was delivered according to a timetable, although they recognised that certain things might need to be covered or discussed. However, they felt that if people were provided with enough information at their first fitting, then follow-up services could focus on problems or difficulties that group members were experiencing. They also liked the idea of having a flexible structure and materials prepared for distribution that could help with real life and real-time problems.

Conclusion

Despite its limitations this study demonstrates that older people with age-related hearing problems crave better information and are amenable to group-rehabilitation processes geared toward helping them to adapt to hearing aids. The proposed group approach outlined in this paper offers a potentially cost-effective alternative to current service models, and its further development and evaluation are recommended. Finally, when bringing together research participants with a shared problem and strong common needs, the potential for the development for mutual aid should be factored into research design, and researchers should plan for ways to deal with any dilemmas posed by the need to collect data while attending to the emergent needs of potentially vulnerable people who are participating in that research.

Acknowledgement

We acknowledge the assistance of RNID Scotland who funded this study.

References

Abrahamson, J. (1991). Teaching coping strategies: A client education approach to aural rehabilitation. *Journal of the Academy of Rehabilitative Audiology*, 24, 43-53.

Abrahamson, J. (2000). Group audiologic rehabilitation. *Seminars in Hearing*, 21(3), 227-233.

Abrams, H., Chisolm, T. H., & McArdle, R. (2002). A cost-utility analysis of adult group audiologic rehabilitation: Are the benefits worth the cost? *Journal of Rehabilitation Research and Development*, 39(5), 549-558.

Abrams, H. B. Hnath-Chisolm, T., Guerreiro, S. M. & Ritterman, S. I. (1992). The effects of intervention strategy on self-perception of hearing handicap. *Ear and Hearing,* 13(5), 371-377.

Alberti, P. W., Pichora-Fuller, M. K., Corbin, H., & Riko, K. (1984). Aural rehabilitation in a teaching hospital: Evaluation and results. *Annals of Otolaryngology Rhinology & Laryngology,* 93, 589-594.

Andersson, G., Melin, L. Scott, B. & Lindberg, P. (1995). An evaluation of a behavioural treatment approach to hearing impairment. *Behavior Research Therapy,* 33(3), 283-292.

Baker, C. (2002). Caring for patients with hearing impairments. *Dermatology Nursing,* 14(1), 49-52.

Benyon, G. J., Thornton, F. L., & Poole, C. (1997). A randomised, controlled trial of the efficacy of a communication course for first time hearing aid users. *British Journal of Audiology,* 31, 345-351.

Binnie, C. A. (1977). Attitude changes following speech reading training. *Scandinavian Audiology,* 6, 13-19.

Brickley, G. J., Cleaver, V.C.G., & Bailey, S. (1996). An evaluation of a group follow-up scheme for new NHS hearing aid users. *British Journal of Audiology,* 30, 307-312.

Brooks, D. N. (1981). Use of post-aural aids by National Health Service Patients. *British Journal of Audiology,* 15, 79-86.

Brooks, D. N. & Johnson, D. I. (1981). Pre-issue assessment and counselling as a component of hearing-aid provision. *British Journal of Audiology,* 15, 13-19.

Bizner, S. M. (2002). The future of the past in aural rehabilitation. *Seminars in Hearing,* 22(1), 3-12.

Cunningham, D. R. (1996). Hearing aid selection counseling: Helping patients make decisions. *The Hearing Journal,* 49(5), 31-49.

Delbecq, A., & Van de Ven, A.H. (1971) A Group process model for problem identification and program planning. *Journal of Applied Behavioral Science,* 7, 466-492.

Delb, W., D'Amelio, R., Boiston, C. J., & Plinkert, P. K. (2002). Evaluation of the tinnitus retraining therapy as combined with a cognitive behavioural group therapy. *HNO,* 50(11), 997-1004. (original in German)

Dillon, H., Koritschoner, E., Battaglia, J., Lovegrove, R., Ginis, J., Mavrias, G., Carnie, L., Ray, P. Forsythe, L., Towers, E., Goulias, H. & Macaskill, F. (1991). Rehabilitation effectiveness II: Assessing the outcomes for clients of a national hearing rehabilitation program. *Australian Journal of Audiology,* 13(2), 68-82.

Elman, R. J. & Bernstein-Ellis, E. (1999). The efficacy of group communication treatment in adults with chronic aphasia. *Journal of Speech, Language, and Hearing Research,* 42(2), 411-419.

Gatehouse, S. (2003). Rehabilitation: Identification of needs, priorities and expectations, and the evaluation of benefit. *International Journal of Audiology, 42*(2S), 77-83.

Gatehouse, S., Stephens, S.D. G., Davis, A. C. & Bamford, J. (2001). *Good Practice Guidance for Adult Hearing Aid Fittings and Services.*

Gianopoulous, I., Stephens, D., & Davis, A. (2002). Follow up of people fitted with hearing aids after adult hearing screening: The need for support after fitting. *British Medical Journal, 325,* (August), 471.

Hawkins, D. B. (2005). Effectiveness of counselling-based adult group aural rehabilitation programs: A systematic review of the evidence. *Journal of the American Academy of Audiology,* 16, 485-493.

Hickson, L., Timm, M., & Worrall, L. (1999). Hearing aid fitting: Outcomes for older adults. *Australian Journal of Audiology,* 21(1), 9-21.

Hickson, L., Timm, M., & Worrall, L. (1999). Hearing aid fitting: Outcomes for older adults. *The Australian Journal of Audiology,* 21(1), 9-21.

Hickson, L. & Worrall, L. (2003). Beyond hearing aid fitting: Improving communication for older adults. *International Journal of Audiology,* 42 (2S), 84-91.

Hickson, L., Worrall, L., Yiu, E., & Barnett, H. (1996). Planning a communication education program for older people. *Educational Gerontology,* 22, 257-269.

Hogan, A. (2001). *Hearing rehabilitation for deafened adults: A psychosocial approach.* London: Whurr Publishers.

Huang, Q. & Tang, J. (2010). Age-related hearing loss or presbycusis. *European Archives of Oto-Rhino-Laryngology,* 267(8), 1179-1191.

Jordan, F. M., Worrall, L. E., Hickson, L. M. H., & Dodd, B. J. (1993). The evaluation of intervention programmes for communicatively impaired elderly people. *European Journal of Disorders of Communication,* 28, 63-85.

Kelly, T. B., Schofield, I., Booth, J., & Tolson, D. (2006). The Use of Online Groups to Involve Older People in Influencing Nursing Care Guidance. *Groupwork,* 16(1), 69-94

Kricos, P. B. (1997). Audiologic rehabilitation for the elderly: A collaborative approach. *Journal of the Academy of Rehabilitative Audiology,* 30(2), 10-19.

Kricos, P. B., Holmes, A. E., & Doyle, D. A. (1992). Efficacy of a communication training program for hearing-impaired elderly adults. *Journal of the Academy of Rehabilitative Audiology,* 25, 69-80.

Laplante-Levesque, A., Hickson, L. & Worrall, L. (2010). Rehabilitation of older adults with hearing impairment: A critical review. *Journal of Aging and Health* 22(2), 143-153.

Norman, G., George, C. R., & McCarthy, D. (1994). The effect of pre-fitting counselling on the outcome of hearing aid fittings. *Scandinavian Audiology, 23,* 257-263.

Norman, G., George, C. R., Downie, A., & Milligan, J. (1995). Evaluation of a communication course for new hearing aid users. *Scandinavian Audiology, 24,* 63-69.

Northern, J. & Beyer, C. M. (1999) Reducing hearing aid returns through patient education. *Audiology Today,* 11(2), 10-11.

Ross, M. (1997). A retrospective look at the future of aural rehabilitation. *Journal of the Academy of Rehabilitative Audiology, 30,* 11-28.

Shulman, L. (1999). *The Skills of Helping Individuals, Families, Groups, and Communities* (4th edition). Itasca, IL: F.E. Peacock, Publishers.

Steinberg, D. M. (2004). *The Mutual-Aid Approach to Working with Groups: Helping People Help One Another* (2nd ed.). Binghampton, NY: Haworth Press.

Smaldino, S. E. & Smaldino, J. J. (1988). The influence of aural rehabilitation and cognitive style disclosure on the perception of hearing handicap. *Journal of the Academy of Rehabilitative Audiology, 21,* 57-64.

Taylor, K. S. & Jurma, W. E. (1999). Study suggests that group rehabilitation increases benefit of hearing aid fittings. *The Hearing Journal,* 52(9), 52-54.

Timonen, V. (2008). *Ageing Societies: A Comparative Introduction.* Maidenhead: Open University Press.

Tolson, D. (1997). Age-related hearing loss: A case for nursing intervention. *Journal of Advanced Nursing,* 26(6), 1150-1157.

Tolson, D., Schofield, I., Booth, J. & Kelly, T. B. (2007). Partnerships in Best Practice: Advancing Gerontological Care in Scotland. In M. Nolan, E. Hanson, G. Grant, & J. Keady (Eds), *User Participation Research in Health and Social Care: Voices, Values and Evaluation* (pages 33-49). Maidenhead: Open University Press.

Worrall, L. E. & Hickson, L. M. (2003). *Communication disability in aging: From prevention to intervention.* New York: Thomson Delmar Learning.

Worrall, L., Hickson, L., Barnett, H. & Yiu, E. (1998). An evaluation of the *Keep on Talking* program for maintaining communication skills into old age. *Educational Gerontology, 24,* 129-140.

9

Participatory research and evidence-based practice for rape survivor groups:

Implications for practice and teaching

Shantih Clemans & Susan Mason

Summary

An evidence-based group work model is especially useful as a clinical model when combined with participatory action research. When groups are envisioned, planned and formed in a participatory format, the outcomes can contribute to a clinically useful group work approach. Simultaneously, the process serves two functions; it brings about a positive therapeutic group and it encourages support for a larger community. In order to best serve rape survivors, practitioners can adopt an evidence-based position that generates data on the most effective strategies with rape survivors as well as on the first-hand experience of sexual assault. Students of group work and trauma can benefit from learning this model in the classroom, although there are challenges faced in teaching evidence-based group work (Pollio & Macgowan, 2010). Through a review of current literature on evidence-based group work practice, the authors generated a model of practice that combines evidence-based strategies with a participatory research framework (Mason & Clemans, 2008). Using updated literature and new themes from the groups, this paper illustrates the therapeutic power of groups for rape survivors that can be magnified by adding participatory research methods as an evidence-generating technique.

Use of groups for participatory research

The participatory research model has been used mostly in community organization projects where there is collaboration between the research leader(s) and the participants. The level of participation in the design and implementation of research projects varies depending on the research goal and by who initiates the project. Participatory research uses multiple design methods, including ethnography, formal and informal interviewing, and focus groups, to collect, interpret, and act upon data. Typically, the research involves an action plan and is often referred to as *action research* (Reason & Bradbury, 2006). Most commonly, participatory research applies to community organization projects (Jason, Keys, Suarez-Balcazar, Taylor, & Davis, 2004; Mora & Diaz, 2004; Reason & Bradbury, 2006) where it creates empirical databases through the collaborative efforts of participants and researchers. Numerous examples include Garcia's (2003) work on alcohol use among transnational Mexican farm workers and Dullea's (2006) research on women in communities for First Nation natives in Canada.

The use of participatory research as a clinical intervention has attracted less attention but nevertheless is shown to be a powerful means of creating valid data (Miller & Mason, 2002; Schein, 2006). Schein (2006) proposes a model where the clinician involves the client in the inquiry process to improve the data quality. In doing so, the client provides more valid data and the clinician is better able to provide an intervention that matches the client problem. Although Schein did not specify the use of groups in this process, his model fits well with groupwork. Miller and Mason (2002) used a participatory model with patients diagnosed with first-episode schizophrenia. In their work patients diagnosed with schizophrenia disorders designed a project in which they contributed their life experiences in the form of narrative statements. These narratives became a prominent part of a book that also included chapters on medications, research, benefits and other topics of interest for newly diagnosed people and their families to learn about the illness.

Others have both used and advocated for participatory and action-oriented research in social work groups in which healing is an important clinical goal (Alpeter, Schopler, Galinsky, & Pennell, 1999; Malekoff, 1994).

Evidence-based practice
and participatory research

Evidence-based practice and participatory research are related in that both require a carefully outlined protocol, a researchable question, and a thorough search for previous research. In both, a chosen intervention must fit the clients' needs and clients must be fully informed and ideally be active partners in finding the right intervention (Gambrill, 2005). In evidence-based practice, it is rare that any one or group of research studies will fit the exact needs of a client or a group. It is for the group leader to determine which aspects of any given evidence-based intervention is useful in each unique client situation (Pollio & Macgowan, 2010). In participatory research, the group members make the decision about the correct intervention with the assistance of the group leader (Stringer, 2007).

Generally, evidence, in evidence-based practice, is thought to be best when the samples are representative of populations and sufficiently large to encourage replication and generalization (Rosenthal, 2006). The use of smaller samples in focused qualitative studies have typically been ignored in evidence-based practice databases. This has brought about substantial criticism from those working with groups (Gambrill, 2005; Mason & Clemans, 2008; Pollio & Macgowan, 2010; Proctor & Rosen, 2006). Critics have called for the inclusion of qualitative studies and local evidence as sometimes necessary for devising interventions that have a 'goodness of fit' for clients (Gambrill, 2005; Proctor & Rosen, 2006). Pollio and Macgowan (2010) posit that evidence is gained through a systematic collection of data that both confirms and aids in future interventions within a reasonable degree of certainty. They view group leaders as potential scientists, '...testing out solutions derived from best available evidence and using the results from testing a hypothesis to guide further inquiry' (p. 198). Mason and Clemans (2008) suggest that groups in a participatory framework create valid evidence within the context of a therapeutic group. They write of the healing value in group derived evidence for both the participatory group and potentially for future groups. For them, the group mission of disseminating healing experiences for others to benefit from becomes a healing intervention itself.

The usefulness of group stories with rape survivors

To restate, we propose that stories that are generated by group members become evidence that can pave the way for building a compendium of strategies for healing. These strategies have been shown to work with individual group members and the sharing of these healing experiences in turn re-affirms and documents the process of healing. A recent meta-analysis of well-established interventions that helped heal young people who have suffered from sexual abuse confirms that cognitive behavioral therapy that includes narratives works well in individual treatment and with families (Silverman, Ortiz, Viswesvaran, Burns, Kolko, Putnam, & Amaya-Jackson, 2008). We suggest that a cognitive model that focuses on a participatory action plan using narratives as part of the healing work will have a positive effect on group participants. We further believe that when groups produce a product (manuscript, video, song, etc.) that is based on their own life experiences, they are inviting the next group to contribute and so on, until a well formulated plan for healing emerges (Mason & Clemans, 2008). Additionally, the stories give to those less familiar with the trauma associated with rape a valid and in-depth understanding of how people experience the violence perpetrated against them.

We use the term stories and narratives interchangeably in this article. Researchers mostly refer to stories as narratives but they are really stories or descriptions of life events. In this case the stories are about how the group participants experienced rape survival. Stories provide valuable information because they are data most closely related to what really happened. Action research emphasizes the collection of subjective data so that according to its early proponent, Lewin (1948/1997), the participants' world could be better understood. More recently, Dullea (2006) demonstrated the benefit of telling and sharing stories for support and healing from sexual violence among women in an aboriginal community in Canada.

The participatory research model and research on rape survivors

The few articles in the literature that have used a participatory model with survivors of sexual violence have employed narratives as a prominent intervention. Campbell (2002) suggested that we already know about the prevalence of rape, and its violent nature but we know less about the survivor's experiences. She proposed, 'If we provide opportunities for survivors to talk about what has happened to them... we can bring their experiences to light' (p. 120).

Participatory research has several key themes (Alpeter, Schopler, Galinsky, & Pennell, 1999; Alvarez & Gutierrez, 2001), all of which are particularly relevant to research on rape. These themes include the fusion of research and practice, consciousness raising and empowerment, and telling the rape 'story.' Additionally, the protocol requires the sharing of power dynamics between the research participants and the researcher. A focus on social change is a hallmark of participatory action research. These themes are discussed and illustrated with examples from rape survivor groups that we have worked with during the past several years. The narratives are examples of what may happen in a participatory research project with rape survivors. We reviewed the clinical notes and report on thematic group exchanges in the aggregate. Although no narrative is in the members' exact words, the narratives represent how the members addressed various issues and serve as examples of how participatory research can be helpful in both the creation of new knowledge and in healing.

The participatory research model protocol

The model has been designed using the following steps to determine the process:

1. A literature review is conducted to determine if systematic reviews of the planned intervention are available. All empirical studies are noted.
2. A specific plan for generating new data is put into place, with group leaders/researchers trained and all group members consenting to

the process ahead of time.
3. The participatory research model is presented to the group and the members and group leader discuss and agree to the rules and parameters of the project.

At the end of the group cycle (12-18 weeks is common) the goal of the project is for members to create a record of their achievements (for example a manual, a book or a video). Future groups can then make use of and benefit from the knowledge and ultimately, evidence. For knowledge to become evidence, information needs to be 'systematically acquired, and critically reviewed for its research merit' (Pollio & Macgowan, 2010, p. 201). Through the structured process in participatory groups, knowledge becomes evidence when it is re-worked and refined by group members. As the evidence is disseminated, future groups may add or suggest changes based on their experiences. This will lead to further validation of evidence.

Participatory research has several key processes (Alpeter et al., 1999; Alvarez & Gutierrez, 2001), all of which are particularly relevant to research on sexual abuse. The processes of participatory research include the fusion of research and practice, consciousness raising and empowerment, the shifting of the power dynamics between the research participants and the researcher, and the potential for social change brought about by the model (Mason & Clemans, 2008).

Because of its emphasis on shared power and passing knowledge on to others in similar circumstances, the combined model of participatory research and evidence-based practice has particular usefulness with groups of adult sexual assault survivors who commonly struggle with a loss of personal power. The groups indicate the usefulness of the model in that members experienced the group across these concepts:

1. Duality of group purpose: Fusing research and practice
2. Consciousness raising and empowerment
3. Telling the rape 'story'

Participatory research processes and emerging themes

What follows are selected group vignettes that illustrate participatory processes and emerging themes. The purpose of including these vignettes is to demonstrate what participatory research group sessions may be like. The processes and themes are illustrated with group interactions and commentaries that underscore their meaning and direction. The themes come from the authors' direct work with rape survivors. The vignettes are composites of potential sessions where the participatory model is applied.

Participatory research fuses research and practice

A participatory research group always begins with an open discussion of the dual purpose. This particular group would require pre-screening. Rape survivor groups with a sole therapeutic purpose provide members with opportunities to share their trauma experiences in a safe and supportive atmosphere. In a participatory research group, members are engaged in both research and therapy. They need to be fully informed and need to consent to the group's dual purpose: research and therapy, as seen in the following example:

Group Leader: Welcome everyone. We have come together to be part of a unique group. This group has two purposes. One is to provide you with a safe environment to share your experiences and feelings about rape, as well as your experiences with support people. The second purpose is to conduct research. Through your participation and honest sharing of what happened to you, we will all learn more about the experience of rape and what has helped or harmed you in your recovery. We may decide to tape record our discussions in order to have a record of what we learned together. This will serve as a living document to be passed on to future groups to help others in their healing. Also what you share here can help people who have not experienced rape, to better understand what you have gone through. All shared experiences will remain confidential and no names will be attached. This is a voluntary group and if at any time you feel that you cannot continue, you may leave without any further discussion or penalty. Any questions or thoughts about what I just said?

Theresa: So, this group is to help us feel better but it's also about helping others learn from what we have gone through.

Group Leader: That's right.

In accepting the dual role attributed to the group, members embark upon a unique mission and this provides each member with the potential of feeling 'special.' Once the group is formed and consents are given, the group readies itself for taking part in the processes of participatory research.

Consciousness raising and empowerment

Consciousness-raising emphasizes a heightened awareness, often through discussion among peers, of the particular pain of sexism and of the desire to improve society on the basis of this changed awareness. This dynamic process helps survivors realize that they are not the sole cause of their oppression and distress and that, in the case of rape, there are other forces at work, such as socially sanctioned male privilege (Israeli & Santor, 2000; Nes & Iadicola, 1989). Participatory research in rape survivor groups precipitates consciousness-raising by assigning the group a purpose beyond that of a place to express feelings; it becomes a way of placing feelings in the context of the social structure and then using the project as a way of taking action. Action can be defined as writing a book that will help other survivors, participating in a speak-out, or using evidence for lobbying for improved sexual assault legislation.

Participatory research in rape survivor groups also has the function of empowering members through fostering the 'telling of the story' and through encouraging members to document and transmit what helped them heal after the rape. A group leader may begin the group process by posing research questions, such as: what do you have in common as survivors of rape? What are your differences? What has been most helpful to you in the days and weeks following the rape? What has been least helpful? What are your hopes for your recovery? What would you like others in your situation to learn from you?

In the following vignette, the group leader guides the members through a process where they talk about their feelings and experiences after the rape. This simultaneous sharing and generating data has an empowering function for the members as they remain in control of the process and assert their expertise, based on their own experiences. The goal is for their experiences to live on and grow through written documentation that will ultimately aid others. To achieve this goal, the group process needs to be repeated over time and carefully evaluated in order for the knowledge generated from the members to actually become evidence.

Group Leader: An important aspect of our work together is to help us understand from each other what was helpful or unhelpful after the rape. This information is important for two reasons. One: we can begin to learn from each other about our experiences. Second, you may be able to make recommendations to pass on to future rape survivors and people who provide support to survivors, such as therapists. Now is your chance to impact our understanding of what can really help or hurt after a trauma such as rape. Does anyone have any thoughts?

Ariella: Well, I guess I'll go first. This is still hard for me to talk about. After I was raped last year, I felt like everyone in my life was trying to be supportive but they were tiptoeing around me, afraid to upset me even more. I didn't find that helpful because I really wanted and needed to talk about what happened and the silence from everyone made me feel worse, like something was wrong with me.

Reba: I kinda felt the same way. I was staying with my mother after the rape and she just acted like everything was normal. I was very shaken, crying all the time, afraid. And my mother wanted to be helpful but she didn't really know what to say or do.

Group Leader: OK, thank you both. I am going to stop here for a moment to make sure I understand what you are saying, and please correct me if I am wrong. The rape was of course a painful experience—traumatic in and of itself, but afterwards, Ariella and Reba, you felt even more pain because people in your lives did not really know what to say or how to help. This silence, as you say, made you feel even worse. Did I get that right?

Ariella: Yes.

Reba: Uh-huh.

Group Leader: I am wondering if anyone else had a similar experience to share?

Maddy: I felt like I was targeted as this 'sick person.' This was after I told a few people that I trusted. I felt they never looked at me the same again.

Sharon: Yeah, I hear you. I wish I had never said anything. I really regret it now. My husband never got over it. I feel like he blames me even though he says he doesn't. I wish I could just turn back the clock.

Group Leader: OK, I'm going to stop you again to make sure I understand what you are saying. For some of you, telling others about your rape and dealing with their reactions was especially painful. Sharon said that she regrets ever telling at all. Let me ask you to think about what you would tell family or friends when they hear that someone they love has been raped. What should they say or do?

Maddy: The most important thing is to believe that person, no matter what.

Cara: Yeah. And maybe say something like, 'Do you want to talk about what happened?' because some people want to talk about what happened and others don't. But people should have the choice and to not be shut out.

Kelly: People are so afraid to hear about bad things. I would say to someone that the best thing you can do is just listen. Maybe I'll want to tell my story and maybe I won't, but just listen.

Group Leader: Okay, so you are recommending that support people—family, friends—give the survivor a choice about whether she wants to tell the story, but be open to her, no matter what. Blaming is not helpful and silence around the facts of the rape is also not helpful. It is up to the survivor what she tells or not.

By allowing the members to share and generate their experiences of what was helpful and not helpful after their rapes, the group process serves an empowering and consciousness raising function. Members feel ownership over their experiences with support people. The group leader encourages members to explore their own trauma experiences within an emotional context. By telling their stories post-rape, group members can begin to form narratives that become qualitative data on how rape survivors interpret their experiences with support people.

Telling the rape 'story'

Telling the story of rape, from beginning to end, with associated feelings is a crucial therapeutic milestone for many survivors (Knight, 2010). By learning about the meaning survivors attribute to this story telling, support people and professionals in the trauma field can be better informed as to best navigate this process with care. Also it is important to recognize the various meanings telling the story can hold for different people; some may want to share, others are reluctant for their own personal reasons. A group that has a therapy/research purpose gives members the opportunity to discuss their experiences with telling their rape stories, also known as trauma narratives (Knight, 2010). What does it mean to a rape survivor to tell what happened on that fateful day? Are these stories empowering? Harmful to listeners? Is this narrative process necessary for everyone?

As seen in the following illustration, telling the story can be empowering and meaningful to the rape survivors in this group. Telling the story, unique to each member, has the benefit of clearing up misperceptions and myths about the rape. Also, members can attach their feelings to the facts of their rapes. On the other hand, some members are reluctant to share their stories for a host of complex reasons. Here, the worker wears two hats: as a therapist offering support and sparking mutual aid among the members; and as a co-researcher, helping members use their experiences as data to be passed on to help others in similar circumstances.

Group Leader: It is helpful to hear from many of you that you would have liked to have the opportunity to 'tell your story,' or share your personal narrative about what happened to you and how you felt. This experience of telling what happened to you may be important for family and friends who want to help but may not really know how to. Let's talk about what telling your unique story means to you. Is there a power associated with this telling? Do some of you avoid telling what happened, and why?

Marjorie: Wow, that's a hard thing for me to think about. I was raped by an ex-boyfriend. Everyone, I think, assumed it was no big deal because you know, we had been intimate before. But for me, that was the worst part—the betrayal of trust. So I wanted people in my life to know that it is not just about sex. It's about, for me anyway, the betrayal of trust. Telling my whole story would get to this point, I think.

Group Leader: So, for you, being raped by an ex-boyfriend, you would want people to understand that you were betrayed beyond the sexual nature of the crime.

Marjorie: Yeah, I think people don't get that because rape is still viewed as sex to outsiders.

Robin: I can relate. Look, I was raped by a stranger. He held me up at gunpoint. I swear, he almost killed me. The sexual part was awful, but so was almost dying (breaks down crying).

Group Leader: Thank you for sharing that. I can see how hard it is for you. Do you feel that people in your life don't understand how close to death you came?

Robin (calming down): Yeah, it's like rape is just sex so what is the big deal? And my boyfriend does not get it. He is totally fixated on the sex part, not that I almost died, but that I was 'with' some other guy. That's all he thinks about. I don't know how to have him see the whole picture.

Group Leader: It seems that part of helping outsiders to see the whole picture, as you say, is for you to tell your story, from start to finish, including all the feelings that go along with it. This telling might help you too. How do you all feel about this?

Sharon: Well, I can't imagine telling every detail to my family. I would be too embarrassed and I wouldn't want to cause them anymore pain.

Kelly: But why do you feel you need to protect them? You didn't do anything wrong. I want to tell my story to anyone who will listen.

Sharon: I know I didn't do anything to cause what happened, but maybe I do blame myself still.

Group Leader: Are some of you worried that if you tell your stories, from start to finish, people who are listening may find reasons to blame you?

Robin: Maybe. I had not thought about it that way. I know that I hold back from sharing too much.

Marjorie: I can see why it would be important to talk about what happened but it is really hard for me because I don't want to relive that awful day. I just want to move on.

Group Leader: Okay. Thank you everyone for offering your thoughts on the process of telling the story. It seems that for some of you, talking opening, with feelings attached, has been helpful to your healing, depending on who you tell and how they react. By telling everything, you may be filling in the gaps for family or friends who have been making assumptions that were untrue.

Robin: Yeah—like it's all about sex.

Group Leader: Yes. That is a common misconception about sexual assault. Also for others like you, talking in detail about what happened may be traumatic in and of itself, since the 'telling' may bring you back to that day and to all the associated emotions. (Pause). Because we are gathering data or information in this group, what suggestions could you make to other rape survivors about 'telling the story?'

Theresa: I think telling about the rape is best done in therapy or here, in this group, with people who have been through it and understand.

Marjorie: I know it is important to not keep it all inside, but I just would not want to tell any stranger on the street. Can you imagine?

Group Leader: Okay. What you are saying is that telling the story has value depending very much on who is listening—a group, a therapist, or a family member. Did I get that right?

Cara: It's also about why you want or need to tell. It has to be for the right reasons, not to shock or hurt someone.

Ariella: I know for me, I would have to prepare and be really ready to go down that road. It can't be spontaneous. That could be dangerous.

Group Leader: So the telling of the story can be an important experience for many reasons. However, from what I am hearing, you, as survivors, need to be emotionally ready to share the details and you have to be clear the reasons why you are sharing. You need to be in charge of this process. The telling needs, I think, to be most helpful to you in your recovery. Did I get that right?

This example shows the group leader working carefully with the members to have them consider their feelings about sharing personal trauma narratives, to whom and under what circumstances. The dual purpose of the group is evident in the worker helping members talk with each other in a supportive, non-judgmental and caring manner. At the same time, through direct questioning and clarification, the group leader helps the group generate data through the activity of creating and sharing personal narratives. A parallel process is at play here; the group is discussing the concept of sharing personal narratives, at the same time, they are creating a narrative of this process. This data can be used to make recommendations to future rape survivors and support people in individual, group, and community contexts. A group may choose to record sessions or to document discussions through note-taking and transcription, create a living document in the form of a book or a video. The group created product can be passed on to future groups, organizations, or to the public.

Discussion

A participatory research model that uses groups can be both a medium for healing and a way to generate knowledge--and eventually evidence. In this example the group of rape survivors are just beginning to understand the value of the dual mission, healing and creating evidence. Getting group members ready for this process is complex. Members of a participatory research group must agree to the group's dual purpose and must be fully along in their personal recovery to be able to contribute to a group that is not solely therapeutic and one that makes demands on members to be more than group members. The movement from being a primarily therapy group to one with a dual mission can take time and calls for skill and sensitivity on the part of the group leader. At a crucial point in the process, the group 'will get it', that they are in charge and the leader is there to serve as a resource and mediator when needed. When this happens, action or participatory research takes place and shared experiences take on a special meaning. They become data, to be discussed, re-worked, and refined as valid evidence to be passed on.

Clinical implications

This model has implications for clinical practice. Because this group is a forum for generating evidence of the first hand experiences of rape survivors, those who work with these survivors gain knowledge into what makes a meaningful intervention for survivors. The group also can offer helpers (social workers and others) information on useful healing techniques. By being part of a group such as the one described in this article, members are able to have a unique opportunity to help change public perceptions of rape and rape recovery. In groups where sessions are recorded and evidence is turned into a product there is a permanency attached to the group. For group members, this can increase self esteem and feelings of being in control. However, group leaders need also to be aware of potential feelings of responsibility for the contents of the product that can bring about anxiety. Once the project's action product is complete, members may require additional sessions to process feelings about their contributions, even when there is anonymity. The fact that future groups and a variety of 'others' may benefit from their work can be both satisfying and frightening. Leaders need to check this out.

Educational implications

Evidence-based group work is a subject that is increasingly common in schools of social work. Social work students can benefit from being exposed to participatory models of research and practice. However, there are challenges and complexities inherent in this model. Questions arise such as: How can evidence-based practice be effectively taught to students in the field? What challenges do teachers and students face? How is this model different from other group work models? How does the classroom environment contribute the effective teaching of this model?

Teaching the combined evidence-based/participatory research model is an ambitions undertaking for faculty, but one that is well worth the challenge. Educating MSW-level students, for example, takes patience, creativity and thoughtfulness on the part of a teacher. This model can be incorporated in several courses across the social work curriculum. Most often, evidence-based practice content and process will appear in social group work methods courses where students are exposed to theory, skills, and group simulations. Another way of teaching the model would be to infuse it into topical courses. In the case of rape survivors, courses on practice with trauma and interpersonal violence would be a good fit. A course focusing on the social forces, abuse dynamics and current treatment approaches for clients affected by rape and other forms of intimate violence would benefit from its inclusion. The model also lends itself to a variety of topics including recovery from addictions, emotional problems, and family issues, just to name a few.

An additional area of the social work curriculum where this model would find a home is a course specifically on evidence-based practice, an increasingly common addition to social work curricula. Pollio and Macgowan (2010) call for an integrated approach to teaching evidence based group work that combines theory, group models, evidence, a practice situation, and supervision. Infusing group processes into traditionally non-groupwork courses is a subject worth pursuing for curriculum writers. Students often learn best when they experience hands-on skill developing exercises. Group leadership skills have an important place in most practice courses.

A classroom environment that mirrors a 'real' group, mindful of appropriate classroom boundaries that focus on education not personal therapy for students, can powerfully contribute to student learning. Participating in a 'classroom community,' allows students to feel safe and competent to participate in group simulations. Pollio and Macgowan (210) note, 'Ongoing simulations of groups can allow students to participate in situations where they can directly practice their skills and observe others making their own experiments in practice situations' (p. 206).

Above all, students exposed to instruction in evidence-based group work and participatory action research benefit from sharpened critical thinking and intuitive skills. Being able to understand current research findings, apply these findings to their particular groups, and foster knowledge-generating techniques through groups that involve members as co-researchers, contributes to the richness of theirs and our understanding of social phenomena, in this case, of rape and rape recovery for survivors. Employing planning, perseverance, and thoughtfulness in teaching, learning, and applying a combined evidence-based group/participory research model presents a dynamic opportunity for student-practitioners and social work educators alike.

References

Alpeter, M., Schopler, J. H., Galinsky, M. J., & Pennell, J. (1999). Participatory research as social work practice. *Journal of Progressive Human Services,* 10(2), 31-53.

Alvarez, A. R., & Gutierrez, L. M. (2001). Choosing to do participatory research: An example and issues of fit to consider. *Journal of Community Practice,* 9(1), 1-20.

Campbell, R. (2002). *Emotionally Involved: The Impact of Researching Rape.* New York: Routledge.

Dullea, K. (2006). Woman shaping participatory research to their own needs. *Community Development Journal,* 41(1), 65-74.

Gambrill, E. (2005). *Critical Thinking in Clinical Practice: Improving the Quality of Judgments and Decisions* (2nd ed.). Hoboken, NJ: John Wiley.

Garcia, V. (2003). Critical ethnography and substance abuse research among transnational Mexican farmworkers. In J. Mora & D. R. Diaz (Eds.), *Latino Social Policy: A Participatory Research Model* (pp. 119-153). Binghamton, NY: Haworth Press.

Jason, L. A., Keys, C. B., Suarez-Balcazar,Y., Taylor, R. R., & Davis, M. I. (Eds.). (2004). *Participatory Community Research: Theories and Methods in Action.* Washington, DC: American Psychological Association.

Knight, C. (2009). *Introduction to Working with Adult Survivors of Childhood Trauma: Techniques and Strategies.* Belmont, CA: Thompson Brooks/Cole.

Malekoff, A. (1994). Action research: An approach to preventing substance abuse and promoting social competency. *Health and Social Work,* 19, 46-53.

Mason, S.E. & Clemans, S.E. (2008). Participatory research for rape survivor groups: A model for practice. *Affilia: Journal of Women and Social Work,* 23(1), 66-76.

Miller, R. & Mason, S. E. (2002). *Diagnosis Schizophrenia.* New York: Columbia University Press.

Mora, J. & Diaz, D. R. (Eds.). (2004). *Latino Social Policy: A Participatory Research Model.* Binghamton, NY: Haworth Press.

Pollio, D. & MacGowan, M. (2010). The andragogy of evidence-based group work: An integrated educational model. *Social Work with Groups,* 33(2/3), 195-209.

Pollio, D. & MacGowan, M. (2010). From the guest editors: Introduction to evidence-based group work in community settings. *Social Work with Groups*, 33(2/3), 98-101.

Proctor, E. K. & Rosen, A. (2006). Concise standards for developing evidence-based practice guidelines. In A. R. Roberts & K. R. Yeager (Eds.), *Foundations of Evidence-Based Social Work Practice* (pp. 93-102). New York: Oxford University Press.

Rosenthal, R. N. (2006). Overview of evidence-based practices. In A. R. Roberts & K. R. Yeager (Eds.), *Foundations of Evidence-Based Social Work Practice* (pp. 67-80). New York: Oxford University Press.

Silverman, W. K., Ortiz, C. D., Viswesvaran, C., Burns, B. J., Kolko, D. J., Putnam, F. W., Amaya-Jackson, L. (2008). Evidence-based psychosocial treatments for children and adolescents exposed to traumatic events. *Journal of Clinical Child and Adolescent Psychology*, 37, 156-183.

Stringer, E.T. (2007). *Action Research* (3rd ed.). Thousand Oaks, CA: Sage Publications.

10
Relevance of group work's humanistic values and democratic norms to contemporary global crises

Urania Glassman

Introduction:
Group work's humanistic values
and democratic norms and the United
Nations Declaration of Human Rights

Group Work's Humanistic Values and Democratic Norms (Glassman, 2008) serve as a foundation for: a) developing skills of democratic participation, and b) developing interactional skills for bridging cultural barriers. Some of these humanistic values include the following (see Appendix 1 for full listing of humanistic values and democratic norms.)

- The individual is inherently worthy.
- The individual has the right to belong, to be included.
- The individual is responsible to and for others.
- The individual has the right to take part, to be heard.
- The individual has the right to freedom of speech, to freedom of expression.
- The individual is valued for one's difference which is seen as enriching the process.

These humanistic values, and the democratic norms which

operationalize these values, are consonant with the United Nations Declaration of Human Rights (U.N., 1948), and have universal relevancy in the global context. Some of the human rights declarations include:

The freedom, equality and dignity of the individual.

The right to freedom of thought, conscience, religion, without exception and regard to race, sex; religion, national origin, or social position.

The right to... hold opinions without interference and to seek, receive and impart information and ideas through any media and regardless of frontiers.

(U.N., 1948). (See Appendix 2, Excerpts from U.N. Declaration of Human Rights.)

The United Nations Declaration of Human Rights (U.N., 1948) has been considered the benchmark for human rights in the global community, and the template against which human rights violations are scrutinized and defined. The humanistic values and democratic norms of the social work group also provide a related benchmark to the world community by presenting a comparable value base to guide the operationalization of the human rights declaration in the group life of members in all parts of the world.

Issues facing global community

Political factors such as anti-democratic forces, terrorism, threats of war, and lack of tolerance threaten the implementation and realization of humanistic values and democratic norms in group life. As such, these political factors prevent a range of individuals and communities from achieving rights outlined in the U.N. Declaration of Human Rights. Along with oppressive political forces are massive sociological factors. These include world-wide immigration and mass migrations frequently associated with economic issues, and the uprooting of communities due to natural disaster or war which impede the development of social structures in groups and communities built on humanistic values and the human rights perspective.

Addressing these issues through the values and operational base of group work

A variety of social work support groups, community groups, and crisis groups formed in the non political arena can be important vehicles for working with people caught in the throes of political and social crises, through the development of democratic group process as an underpinning for healing. Groups built on social group work's values also have the potential to help members bridge cultural barriers to deal with crises. Groups based on humanistic values and democratic norms can be formed to create laboratories in democracy and valuing difference which give hope to the members.

While social workers with groups may not likely have the power to repair what has been created in the wider political, economic, and social realms, participation in a group based on group work's humanistic values and democratic norms can be reparative and restore hope for people who have escaped traumatic circumstances into newer more hospitable and secure environments where the work of healing can begin. The right of the individual to mental health and well being, recognized by Konopka (1983) as an essential human right, can be fostered in a secure group environment which helps to restore members' well being and mental health.

Illustrative use of humanistic values and democratic norms of social work group for repairing totalitarian experiences

Totalitarian political environments create trauma and population movements which produce millions of refugees and displaced persons worldwide. In 2009, over 36 million persons were identified as populations of concern worldwide by the UN High Commission on Refugees (2010). Support groups for refugees have historically helped alleviate the stress and despair of their members while providing hope for a better future. Mayadas (1982) then Deputy Commissioner of the U.N. High Commission on Refugees which at that time received a

Nobel Peace Prize, describes the use of group work with Viet Nam war refugees to help them find comfort and the support to move on and create new lives. Groups played an important role in one program for South East Asian refugees (Glassman & Skolnik, 1984) whose groups were used to validate and strengthen the connection between refugees and their new home, as well as to explore how to engage with the new culture. In these groups, members who had experienced lack of freedom of speech in a totalitarian and war torn situation were also able to speak freely about those times and the attacks to their freedoms they lived under and endured. The conscious development of democratic norms by practitioners fostered these open expressions. The U.N. Declaration of Human Rights (1948) served as the underpinning.

Kalcher (2001) traces the history after World War II of efforts by social workers and social pedagogues to reactivate humanistic ideas and values in Germany through the initiation of group programs. His presentation describes the development of the 'Hansische Jugendbund,' one of the very first post-WWII examples of a group work agency in the city of Hamburg focused on developing small face to face democratic groups as an antidote to Nazi indoctrination of youth. In a similar vein, Masanek (2001) discusses the practical application of the principles of democratic values in group experience. In her keynote presentation at the annual symposium of the Association for the Advancement of Social Work with Groups in Akron, Ohio, Masanek explored Grace Coyle's concepts and values of group work as these have been applied to responsible citizenship in other countries and cultures, particularly in post WWII Germany and in the present context. This presentation had great impact having occurred one month after September 11, 2001. The effect was chilling because it gave those present pause to wonder about the extent to which ideologues gain access to people's minds by manipulating belief systems to create movement of violence and hatred. Masanek's presentation also fostered positive anticipations by bringing home the value of the democratic group as one antidote for violence, hatred and intolerance.

David (2006) has described the healing power of groups for elderly Holocaust survivors and their younger Rwandan counterparts at Baycrest Center for Geriatric Care in Toronto. In this bi-cultural group work program for survivors of genocide, group members from both populations were able to share with one another the impact on their lives, their children, and their families of having lived through countless atrocities. Rather than despair, hope was furthered through the group process and the older Holocaust survivors had much to offer to younger Rwandans about their own efforts and missteps in dealing with these issues throughout the progression of their lives.

When people are able to come out of themselves and their own cultural or ethnic group, to experience their situations through the mirror of the other who is not from their own circumstances, healing can occur in two ways: the validation that results when the other hears the story, and through the universalization by the other that what has been described was a clear violation of a universal set of human rights. Very often in these types of group settings, the worker represents the role of the 'other,' who validates the experience (Glassman & Skolnik, 1984).

Groups for bridging cultural barriers globally: A paradigm

Group work treatment of dysfunctional social environments is primarily reliant on the social goals or reciprocal model (Papell & Rothman, 1980) as a group work practice paradigm. Individuals are not considered problematic; rather dysfunctional social environments, peer groups, and reference groups, are the origin of members' interactional problems, and the small owned group is the center within which members develop newer coping strategies and communication.

In multicultural groups members are asked to identify social obstacles that they unwittingly use which prevent them from seeing the person before them empathically or realistically without distortion, or from being seen for who they are (Glassman, 2008). In the group treatment situation, distortions are based on psychological factors; in the multicultural group, distortions are based on social factors. Distortions based on psychological and social factors can be modified through face to face contact and opportunity the group affords for the changing of perceptual lenses. Glassman's tools for assessing group members further sheds light on the process by which members stereotype and stigmatize one another, and how the group may be used as an arena for changing perceptual lenses and interactions.

Applying the paradigm

By way of illustration, New York City is a hub of multi-culturalism with so many older generations of immigrants and their adult children, living alongside just as many newer and younger groups, it is hard to catch up with who they are. Toronto is yet another exemplar, as are many of the U.S. large, mid-sized and smaller cities. In fact, it is critical to understand the following fact: mass migrations are not unique North American phenomena. Just witness Europe after the fall of the Soviet Union and the resultant influx of Eastern Europeans into Western Europe, not to mention the huge number of Turks as well as Arabs and Africans from many nations. And turning to Asia, consider the major metropolis of Hong Kong growing from 2 million in 1970 to 5.5 million in 1996 by incorporating Chinese mainland immigrants, many of whom did not even speak the same language. The complex social problems and social imperatives created by these and similar migrations challenged nations to provide housing, employment, and tools for assimilation and peaceful living within the borders for old and new residents.

No sooner did new Yorkers learn about Koreans, Dominicans, many other Hispanic groups, and newer Chinese immigrants, they had to figure out who the brand new Africans were, how to tell the difference between Haitians and Nigerians, and who the Muslim groups represent – Pakistan or an Arab country or an African country, and where exactly a Sikh is from.

New Yorkers generally see this as an opportunity to hear a different language, go to another ethnic parade, and get a new kind of street food before the price goes up when the restaurant opens. This influx of newer ethnic groups is of course evident in schools, and due to the emphasis on multi cultural understanding in the schools, potential conflicts can be converted into learning opportunities. However keeping the peace happens because people make planned efforts to dialogue, to operate within and maintain democratic principles and processes, and to enact them through programs that foster the principles and processes in small group life. When these structures have either broken down or not been developed, the risk of violence is heightened – for example the recent gang related bias attacks on gay youths and immigrants in New York City.

Youth and young adult groups for multi-cultural understanding in school and university settings have been described earlier as an arena for permitting young people to air differences and deal with stereotypes and misinformation which enhances dialogue and understanding (Glassman, 1994). In college and high school groups, members from widely different backgrounds (Russian Jew, Holocaust family, Puerto Rican migrant families, British-African , gay Polish-Turkish American, French university student) representing a range of issues shared common family histories centered on leaving homelands to escape persecution or to escape the persecution of slavery. In one session, maps were used with members to trace their families' migrations and frame their own and each others' understanding.

One programmatic effort using groups for young people has been put forth by the Jewish Community Relations Council (JCRC, 2006). The Bridge Program has been developed for the wide spectrum of urban youth to promote understanding and leadership among New York's high school youngsters. The assumption is that everyone in New York City reflects diversity. Several hundred participate in a city wide program planned by their peer leadership, and also meet regularly in smaller groups to build this effort and promote healthy group and intergroup life in their respective schools and neighborhoods. Democratic group norms focused on respecting difference, free speech and free expression, equality in participation, and rights to take leadership are emphasized, and the program is a learning laboratory to foster these values and norms.

In the offices of local politicians, youth initiatives to address violence and the need for tolerance have abounded. Congressmen Charles Rangel, and Ed Townes, former Manhattan Borough Presidents Ruth Messinger and C. Virginia Fields, Assemblyman Vito Lopez, are among the elected officials who have effectively spearheaded these programs. (It is no accident that Townes, Messinger, Fields, and Lopez are social workers.)

Another program centers on the desire to reaffirm the historical partnership between African Americans and Jews which had found itself on shaky ground as a result of various political factors. Three programs were conducted on Jewish-Black relations (Yeshiva University Wurzweiler School of Social Work, 1999) which brought together leaders in these communities to discuss issues and current efforts to strengthen the historic ties between these communities. Partnerships highlighted included: the coalition in the south among churches and synagogues (Forman, 1999); the Jewish community's 'out of the ashes program' centered on rebuilding southern black churches that had been destroyed by bombings (Schneier, 1999); the basketball league developed in Crown Heights Brooklyn between the Hassidic and Black youth in the aftermath of community riots occurring in the early 1990s; and the group program for African American and Jewish teens in New Jersey (Sweifach, 2008). All of these programs have been built on group work's humanistic values and democratic norms and the U.N. human rights perspective.

Implications

The two group domains presented above -- groups for repairing effects of totalitarianism, and group work programming for bridging cultural barriers – have as their foundation group work's humanistic values and democratic norms. These groups all have the potential to implement the U.N. human rights perspective as an antidote for persons who have been violated by totalitarianism, global conflict, resultant mass migrations or who require education and support in order to learn how to enact these values in their daily lives.

When working with small face to face groups social workers with groups must always be cognizant of and educate themselves to the multiple world contexts represented by the members in their groups. In some cases, groups will focus entirely on healing the ruptures created by intolerant and oppressive environments. In instances where groups have been designed to address other issues, these ruptures will not be immediately obvious. Nonetheless, the group will in fact serve a corrective function for those members who have come from totalitarian or otherwise traumatic political, social and economic situations.

Konopka (1983) wrote that along with freedoms, people had the right to mental health and well being. It is up to social group workers to maintain the vision of group work's meaning in the broader context of human rights, and to accept the responsibility of helping people heal from the many global crises in which they have been. It remains group work's responsibility, albeit daunting, to create environments that support human rights and use humanistic values and democratic norms to foster the achievement of mental health and well being.

References

David, P. (2006) Personal communication, as Coordinator of the Holocaust Resource Project at Baycrest Centre for Geriatric Care, Toronto, Canada.

Devore, W. & Schlesinger, E. (1998) *Ethnic Sensitive Social Work Practice* (5th ed.). NY: Allyn & Bacon.

Forman, Rabbi Lawrence. (1999). Norfolk, VA, Ohef Sholom Temple - Reform Jewish Congregation.

Glassman, U. (2008). *Group Work: A Humanistic and Skills Building Approach* (2nd ed.). Los Angeles, CA: Sage Publications.

Glassman, U. (1995). *Humanistic Group Work as a Model for Providing a Corrective Experience: Groups in Mental Health and for Bridging Cultural Barriers.* Paper presented at the XVII Annual International Symposium of the Association for the Advancement of Social Work with Groups, San Diego, CA., USA.

Glassman, U. (1994). *The Use of Group Work to Promote Multi-Cultural Understanding Among Youth.* Paper presented at the XVI Annual International Symposium of the Association for the Advancement of Social Work with Groups, Hartford, CT, USA.

Glassman, U. & Skolnik, L. (1984). The role of group work in refugee resettlement. *Social Work with Groups,* 7(1) 49-62.

JCRC (2006). Personal communication, Robert Kaplan & Lara Mayouhas. The Intergroup Relations Program develops activities for a spectrum of groups in NYC, Jewish, Asian, African American, Latino, Russian, and has included Arab American and Muslim communities.

Kalcher, J. (2001). *Social Group Work in Germany: An American Import and its Historical Development.* Paper presented at the XXIII Annual International Symposium of the Association for the Advancement of Social Work with Groups, Akron, OH, USA.

Konopka, G. (1983). *Social Group Work: A Helping Process* (3rd ed.). Englewood Cliffs, N.J.: Prentice Hall.

Masanek, I. (2001). The Practical Application of the Principles of Democratic Values in Group Experience. Plenary paper presented at the XXIII Annual International Symposium of the Association for the Advancement of Social Work with Groups, Akron, OH, USA.

Papell, C. & Rothman, B. (1980). Relating the mainstream model of social work with groups to group psychotherapy and the structured group approach. *Social Work with Groups,* 3(2), 5-22.

Schneier, Rabbi Marc (1999). Director of Institute of Multi-Ethnic Understanding.

U.N. High Commission on Refugees (2010). www.unhcr.org/pages/49c3646c4d6.html Global trends.

U.N. (1948). United Nations Declaration of Human Rights. www.un.org/en/documents/udhr/index.shtml .

Yeshiva University Wurzweiler School of Social Work (1999). African Americans and Jews: Three conferences conducted from 1994-1999.

Appendix 1

Humanistic values and democratic norms of the social work group: Excerpts (Glassman, 2008)

Value #1, The individual is inherently worthy

The *norm for valuing vs. devaluing the rights of every member*

Value #2, The individual is responsible to and for others

a) The *norm for caring and mutual aid vs. exploitive relations*

b) The *norm for cooperative vs. competitive relations.*

Value #3, The individual has the right to belong, to be included

a) The *norm for inclusive vs. exclusive relations*

b) The *norm for dealing openly and rationally with prospective members*

c) The *norm for permitting membership to a 'difficult' or 'different' member*

Value #4, The individual has the right to take part, to be heard

The *norm securing and supporting open participation of all*

Value #5, The individual has the right to self determination

a) The *norm fostering equal power distribution*

b) The *norm for opening decision making processes*

c) The *norm for using cooperative programming to enhance members*

Value #6, The group members have the right to an accountable worker

The *norm for directly expressing reactions to worker*

Value #7, The individual has the right to freedom of speech, to freedom of expression

a) The *norm for maintaining open and free communication without reliance on narrow ideology*

b) The *norm for trusting in the expression of feelings*

Value #8, The individual is valued for one's difference which is seen as enriching the process

The *norm for fostering a broad spectrum for deviation vs. conformity*

Value #9, The individual has the right to freedom of choice

a) The *norm fostering freedom to change vs. coercion*

b) The *norm for maintaining an open role system*

Appendix 2

United Nations Declaration of Human Rights (1948): Excerpts

Article 1
All human beings are born free and equal in dignity and rights. They are endowed with reason and conscience and should act towards one another in a spirit of brotherhood.

Article 2
Everyone is entitled to all the rights and freedoms set forth in this Declaration, without distinction of any kind, such as race, colour, sex, language, religion, political or other opinion, national or social origin, property, birth or other status. Furthermore no distinction shall be made on the basis of the political ... status of a country ... to which a person belongs ...

Article 18
Everyone has the right to freedom of thought, conscience, religion ... includes freedom to change religion ...

Article 19
Everyone has the right to freedom of opinion and expression; this right includes the freedom to hold opinions without interference and to seek, receive, and impart information and ideas through any media and regardless of frontiers.

Article 20
1) Everyone has the right to peaceful assembly and association.
2) No one may be compelled to belong to an association.

Article 26
1) Everyone has the right to education. Education shall be free at least in the elementary and fundamental stages. Elementary education shall be compulsory.
2) Education shall be directed to the full development of human personality and to strengthening of respect for human rights and fundamental freedoms. It shall promote understanding, tolerance, and friendship among all nations, racial or religious groups, and shall further the activities of the United Nations for the maintenance of peace.

11

A critical call for connecting students and professional associations

Shirley R. Simon, Joyce A. Webster, Karen Horn

Summary

This paper describes a model aimed at facilitating connections between students and professional associations. It assesses efforts to link Master of Social Work (MSW) students and the Association for the Advancement of Social Work with Groups (AASWG), and delineates the rationale, underlying assumptions, process, impact, and critical factors. Concrete outcomes are identified and suggestions are offered for creating and enhancing connections between these two constituencies.

The authors wish to recognize the invaluable contributions of J. Alejandro Olayo, MSW.

Introduction

The survival of social group work practice and its professional associations as strong, vibrant communities is currently threatened. The leaders of group work are aging and the cadre of dedicated group workers is shrinking due to agency cutbacks, increasing workloads, and a diminished place for group work within the academic social work community. (Birnbaum & Auerbach, 1994; Drumm, 2006; Kurland & Salmon, 2002; Middleman, 1990). Simultaneously, professional associations, and group work associations in particular, are struggling to sustain membership and ensure future growth (Gonzales & Scarcella, 2001; Putnam, 2000). It would seem logical that today's social work students are a potential source of membership and energy. Yet, are we actually reaching out to this constituency in a focused, consistent manner?

A review of the literature clearly documents that students have much to gain by becoming involved in professional associations (Desmond & Symens, 1997; Gonzales & Scarcella, 2001; Knight, 2002; Messmer, 2005). Although the literature indicates that there is some attention paid to this connection in other disciplines (Bloome & Harste, 2001; Desmond & Symens, 1997; Knight, 2002; Messmer, 2005; Royce & Hechtman, 2001), it does not suggest that these connections are being consciously and consistently fostered in the field of social work. With the ever-increasing pressure on social work faculty to engage in research and grant procurement, there is less time and incentive to foster the development of the connection between students and professional associations. It may, however, be imperative that we do just that!

There is a timely opportunity for connection between two constituencies – today's social work students and the voluntary professional associations that advocate for their chosen profession. This linkage may be particularly vital for the Association for the Advancement of Social Work with Groups (AASWG) and group work students at this critical juncture in group work's history. Connecting these two constituencies in a deliberate, multi-pronged approach seems essential for their mutual development.

This paper describes efforts to facilitate the connection between Masters of Social Work Students (MSW) students and AASWG. It delineates the rationale, underlying assumptions, process, impact, and critical factors in its success. Concrete outcomes are reported, and suggestions are offered for creating and enhancing connections between these two constituencies.

The need for connection

To understand the value of linking professional associations and emerging social work professionals, it is essential to first consider the needs and characteristics of both constituencies.

Students' needs

While students' educational needs are met largely through classroom and fieldwork instruction, ongoing professional competence requires connections beyond the academic institution. It is here that professional associations are pivotal. Opportunities for networking, participation in seminars of professional interest, and linkage to job opportunities are but a few of the benefits of association membership (Desmond & Symens, 1997; Gonzales & Scarcella, 2001; Messmer, 2005). Associations foster professional development and leadership, mentorship relationships, career path exploration, access to continuing education through conferences and publications, interaction with practitioners and educators in the field, and the opportunity to contribute to the profession (Desmond & Symens, 1997; Gonzales & Scarella, 2001; Knight, 2002; Messmer, 2005; Royce & Hechtman, 2001).

Furthermore, the need to be supported by a community is especially critical in today's world of isolation and individualization. Social workers, in particular, benefit from one another's support in the current climate of increasing demands, limited resources, and frequent burnout (Bergart & Simon, 2004; Goodman & Munoz, 2004). Professional associations allow students and emerging professionals to participate in and be supported by a community of peers who share common goals and interests. Fostering these connections early in one's career is particularly vital.

Associations' needs

While professional associations provide opportunities to enhance the educational experience of students, associations also rely upon emerging professionals to meet their own objectives. Without an ongoing influx of new dues-paying members and their concomitant energy and ideas, associations would not survive (Goodman & Munoz, 2004). However, as discussed in Putnam's (2000) best-selling book, *Bowling Alone*, individuals today are less likely than in prior decades to join groups, including professional associations. Within social work, professional association membership is curtailed by competition among numerous associations serving similar constituencies, relatively low salaries, reduced need for association-sponsored certification due to the prevalence of state licensure, increasing work and societal demands, and diminished "free" time to participate in voluntary activities. Social work students, therefore, represent a critical constituency. As emerging professionals they are the future leaders of the profession. Gonzales and Scarcella (2001) observe that when students join associations during their academic careers, they will more likely maintain these affiliations as professionals. Thus, tapping this constituency and recruiting their participation, while still students, provides the potential for a long-term membership commitment.

Group work's critical needs

Within group work associations, there is also an urgent need. Group work is currently threatened by the growing number of untrained group work practitioners, increasing focus on a generalist approach within academia, an aging core of group work professionals, and a decrease in the number of self-identified group work agencies and practitioners (Bergart & Simon, 2004; Drumm, 2006; Goodman & Munoz, 2004). Since the standards for social work education have shifted from a method-specific practice to a "generalist" approach, education in social group work has drastically diminished (Birnbaum & Auerbach, 1994; Goodman & Munoz, 2004; Middleman, 1990). Paradoxically, as education has evolved toward a generalist approach, the need for trained group workers has expanded (Goodman & Munoz, 2004). Unfortunately, social group work is increasingly practiced by untrained staff, while those who have training are required to assume additional responsibility without the support of similarly-minded colleagues and supervisors. As Kurland and Salmon (2002) eloquently note:

> Not so long ago, to be a social worker with special commitment to group work placed one in a supportive and stimulating community of colleagues, teachers, supervisors and mentors who shared common values,

understanding, and excitement about group work practice. The method was celebrated and vibrant. That is no longer true today. Those with particular interest in work with groups find it difficult to locate colleagues, teachers, supervisors and mentors with depth of knowledge, understanding and skill who can appreciate, support, and animate their group work efforts. To be a group worker today is to be lonely. (Kurland & Salmon, 2002, p. 10-11).

Given the changing environment for the education and practice of group work, it is not surprising that group work associations are also threatened. For nearly three decades AASWG has been a strong advocate for social group work. However, with the current pressures on group workers, AASWG has found itself struggling with declining membership. In a recent newsletter, the president of AASWG writes,

AASWG's survival is in question. There have been changes over the past few years that have taken a toll. Our membership has slipped...and a small number of committed Board members are carrying a heavy load. (May 2006, 10)

At precisely the time group workers most need a supportive community of similarly minded peers, the association that advocates for their chosen area of practice is struggling to survive.

The role of the academic community

Due to its unique influence with both groups, the academic community can serve as a critical "bridge" in developing the relationship between students and professional associations. Being immersed in an academic community is typically a temporary experience and, upon graduation, the emerging professional often experiences isolation and struggles to forge a relationship with a community of peers (Goodman & Munoz, 2004). To expect students and emerging professionals to independently identify and connect with a professional association is unrealistic. It is, therefore, incumbent upon schools of social work, in conjunction with professional associations, to create structured and easily navigated pathways by which students and associations can "join forces".

Two ways to forge this connection include embedding professional development into the curriculum and providing faculty mentorship to students. Devoting a specific section of the curriculum to orienting students to the value of professional associations can highlight the critical role associations can play in one's professional life. Curriculum can encompass information about association objectives, opportunities for involvement, and the process of presenting at professional conferences (Eitzen, 1988). The faculty mentorship role can include informing students of upcoming conferences, actively promoting student participation in association activities, and modeling and demonstrating the importance of leadership in professional associations (Desmond & Symens, 1997; Knight, 2002). It has long been recognized that having a faculty mentor helps students develop a professional identity. Unfortunately, many of today's graduate students lack the tutelage of a supportive mentor, and the transition from student to professional is left to chance.

The model

Recognizing the complimentary needs of both students and professional associations, as well as the critical role of the academic community, a model was developed at a large Midwestern graduate school of social work to foster connections between these constituencies. Underlying the development of the model were the following key assumptions: 1) The connection between students and professional associations is mutually beneficial; 2) Students will value and participate in association activities if encouraged and supported; 3) The role of the faculty member as the bridge to professional association is critical; 4) The process of connection needs to be relatively simple and clear; 5) Promoting such connections within the classroom is ideal, since student attention and motivation are assured.

Process

Grounded in these assumptions, a group work educator began

by articulating the importance of professional associations to students in her group work courses. The educator invited students to consider submitting abstracts for presentation at the 2005 International Symposium of AASWG. Several students expressed initial interest in the project but voiced reservations about feeling adequately prepared to present at a symposium. Respecting these concerns, the faculty member suggested students collaborate with each other in a small group to jointly prepare an abstract for presentation.

The faculty member then arranged an introductory meeting with interested students and served as the facilitator. She provided further detail about AASWG, oriented the students to the Association, and educated them about the specifics of the upcoming Symposium. Within the context of monthly meetings, the faculty member guided the students through writing and submitting a cohesive abstract. While awaiting notification of the abstract's acceptance, the faculty member shifted the students' focus toward preparing for the presentation. The group continued to meet to organize and edit the presentation, explore how to effectively co-present, and practice how to speak before a professional audience. Throughout the process the faculty member encouraged the students to keep journals detailing their individual responses to the group process. Students were encouraged to share their written reflections with the faculty member and with one another for additional support throughout the project. The students also shared portions of their journal entries as authors of this paper. The abstract was accepted and the students presented at the 2005 AASWG International Symposium, with the faculty mentor serving as the moderator. The presentation was well received with many positive comments from the attendees.

Impact and outcomes

Analysis of the results of this process reveals three major areas of impact: 1) students' enhanced sense of professional competence and self-confidence; 2) increased membership and participation in AASWG; and 3) enhanced institutional appreciation for the value of the student-association connection.

Students' enhanced sense of professional competence and self-confidence

As discussed earlier, student participation in professional association activities can yield significant benefits. The students returned from the Symposium expressing appreciation for the opportunity to network, participate in seminars of professional interest, make contributions to the professional dialogue, explore career opportunities, and belong to a professional community They also expressed increased professional confidence resulting from the realization that they are actually valued by the profession. As one student wrote in her journal,

> *Beginning this process I was unsure I would have anything important to contribute to a professional association and its symposium. However, through the process I have gained confidence in the fact that my youth, energy and perspective are invaluable to the profession. I find it so remarkable that I am able to walk away from this process with an unexpected increased confidence in my skills and assets. I wish every student and new professional could experience the same learning in this way!*

Armed with a newfound sense of professionalism, credibility and belonging, two students felt competent to engage in significant follow-up activities. One assumed a mentoring role for subsequent classes of students interested in becoming involved in AASWG, helping those students to draft abstracts, prepare presentations and become active members in the local chapter. Another developed a research study that surveyed student attitudes regarding professional associations and explored factors that encourage and/or inhibit participation. This study earned a university-wide award recognizing excellence in graduate research. Clearly, participation in this process had a powerful impact on the students' sense of professional competence.

Increased membership and participation in AASWG

Participation in this project also had a beneficial impact on both local and international AASWG activities. The students felt empowered and, in turn, motivated other students to participate in AASWG. The local AASWG chapter benefited from a tripling of its membership and an influx of ideas and energy from new student participants. Not only did the students become active members of the local chapter, but two assumed leadership roles of chapter secretary and committee chair. Student participation in and presentation at the annual AASWG International Symposium also increased substantially. Students from the initial group presented at a subsequent symposium and seven additional students, stimulated by the earlier success, attended the 2006 AASWG Symposium. Two of these students even presented. Because students began to participate in AASWG activities and discussed this involvement both inside and outside of the classroom, faculty members subsequently felt an obligation to participate as well. Hence, chapter meetings also experienced an increase in faculty attendance and contribution. The synergy from both groups led to a revitalization of the chapter and a sense of esprit de corps.

Enhanced institutional appreciation for the value of the student-association connection

Within the culture of the home university, various constituencies - faculty, students and staff - began to recognize the potential impact of linking students and professional associations. Discussions within classes, extracurricular meetings, and research projects stimulated an awareness of the benefits of such connections. The school's appreciation was further enhanced when the student-participant received a university-wide award for research on this topic. In addition, the graduate student association appointed a committee to focus on promoting opportunities for involvement in professional associations.

In order to maintain this momentum, it became clear that these opportunities needed to be institutionalized within the curriculum. With the support of faculty and administration, the faculty mentor proposed, developed and implemented a course module within the group work curriculum designed to foster connections between students and professional associations. All of these initiatives reflect the enhanced institutional recognition of the significance of the student-association connection.

Critical factors

An assessment of this process reveals three key factors leading to its success: 1) the role of the leader, 2) the supportive group process, and 3) the receptivity of the association.

Role of the leader

As illustrated above, the role of the faculty member as catalyst for students' participation was integral to the success of this model. Each student noted the overwhelming importance of the faculty member's encouragement, mentorship and sustained involvement. The faculty member did not simply point the students in AASWG's direction and encourage their participation. Instead, she maintained an ongoing commitment to facilitating their involvement throughout the process. It was critical that she did not just "open the door" but committed herself to helping the students "walk through it". Without the faculty member's active involvement, it is doubtful that the students would have participated as extensively in AASWG and its symposia. As one student's journal entry states:

> *The professor's guidance and facilitation proved to be a key factor in helping me become involved in AASWG. If it were not for the support, commitment and effort of my teacher, I probably would not have participated in the Symposium.*

Supportive group process

Having students learn to prepare and present within the context of a safe, supportive group was another key element in the success of this project. By collaborating with one another to prepare for the Symposium the students and the faculty member developed a strong group identity, which advanced their progress. Each of the students recognized and valued the developing cohesion and each was able to rely on one another for socialization, collaboration and a sense of community. This group process was both valuable and critical to the success of the project. As one of the students reflected:

The single most important aspect of this process has been the ability to work within a small group. Without a doubt, the seemingly simple act of sitting down with a group of like-minded individuals to discuss struggles and fears has had the most impact on my overall experience.

Receptivity of the Association

In developing these connections, the faculty member considered AASWG's non-hierarchical, open, and interactive atmosphere, as well as AASWG's avowed need for new membership and participation. Since AASWG has long been recognized as an inviting community to which new members are readily welcomed and engaged, it seemed logical that this cadre of students would be similarly received. Unlike other professional associations, AASWG's Symposia are gatherings where people can meet and connect without regard for title or professional status. In fact, students reported feeling welcome at both local chapter and Symposia meetings. Their thoughts and suggestions were genuinely considered and, as a result, students gained a sense of value and collegiality. The importance of this receptive environment cannot be overemphasized. As one student was surprised to discover, "For the first time, I felt as if I was a professional with contributions that were valued and respected."

Challenges and limitations

As with any new program, there were obstacles and limitations during development and implementation. Both the students and the faculty mentor identified challenges that must be addressed in order to ensure the success of such a program. These include: 1) students' apprehensions, 2) financial cost of participation, and 3) time commitment and workload.

Students' apprehensions

It is important to recognize that students may be anxious about presenting at an international conference, as most have never done so. They are likely to be unfamiliar with the procedures inherent in participating in a professional symposium. In addition, they may have concerns about the relevance and merit of their presentation as compared to those of more seasoned professionals. It is helpful to be cognizant of these concerns, and support students in recognizing, addressing and handling them. Students also need to be educated about the steps involved in submitting an abstract and preparing a presentation. Clarifying the rigor of the peer review process and its inherent affirmation of the relevance of the presentation is another way to offset students' fears. It is essential to recognize that this orientation should be ongoing, as questions and concerns arise at each stage of the process. If other students or alumni have been through such a program, it may be valuable to have them share their perspectives.

In addition, the role of the small group in allowing for universality and a sense of cohesion is vital. In the context of the group, it is important to allow opportunities for students to discuss their fears and hesitations. By doing so, an environment of trust and openness can be fostered, allowing students to overcome their anxiety and sense of isolation. As one student indicated in her journal,

> With the encouragement of the faculty mentor and the collaborative process of working together to achieve our goals, the Symposium seemed less foreboding.

Financial cost

The cost of participation is another challenge when encouraging students to become involved in professional associations. Factoring in membership dues, transportation, registration, room and board, and miscellaneous expenses, the total financial commitment can be daunting for the typical graduate student. There are, however, numerous ways to reduce the costs associated with participation – volunteering at the symposium to reduce or minimize registration expenses, sharing hotel accommodations with other attendees, seeking alternative off-site lodging, and driving or carpooling to the symposium. Despite such measures, the financial cost of participation may still be a deterrent. Indeed participation was limited by students' financial concerns. Both academic institutions and professional associations need to focus on securing and developing funding to support student participation.

Time commitment and workload

The extent of time and workload commitment on the part of both the students and the faculty member also needs to be considered when implementing such programs. The students were surprised by the time and effort required to develop the presentation. It is important to anticipate that, at various points in the process, students will inevitably question their commitment. Again, group supports, faculty mentorship and encouragement, and a cohesive environment can all minimize the negative effects of the increased workload and time commitment. In addition, enhancing socialization opportunities to foster enjoyment and collegiality can also counteract the stress of the work. Having peers with whom to "divide and conquer" the workload and partialize the problem can also make the process less intimidating.

Similarly, faculty are likely to question the time and effort required for such a project. As with any new program, the initial "seed" energy and time is extensive. This is certainly the case here, as the faculty member was still responsible for maintaining her teaching and research responsibilities and was not receiving additional financial or release time for her efforts. In addition, such projects are not the sort of activities that generally earn academic recognition leading to promotion or tenure. Despite the lack of traditional academic rewards, the faculty member pursued this project because of the intrinsic rewards of developing a close mentorship relationship with students and observing the impact of such a project. For her, it was clear that this was what being an educator was all about – helping students grow and develop into professionals and seeing them make the connections from academic classes to real-life situations.

Conclusion

This project had a significant impact at one academic institution and within one chapter of AASWG. The results breed optimism with regard to enhancing the mutually beneficial connection between students and professional associations. While additional time and evaluation is warranted, initial outcomes seem quite positive. It would be interesting and valuable to see if similar outcomes could be replicated at other schools and within other professional associations.

If the warnings of the leaders in social group work are accurate as to the risks for the future of social group work and its organizations, it is both timely and critical to vigorously pursue linkages between social work students and group work associations. As indicated in this paper, there is much to be done for one another.

The premise for this article is that the student-association connection is mutually beneficial and critical for both constituencies. If this is correct, then there is much AASWG can, and should, do to foster this connection. Programs and incentives aimed directly at student participation within all aspects of the association need to be developed. Some of these include:

- The inclusion of student representatives on the governing board of AASWG. Such representation could enhance the participation, commitment and longevity of the student-association connection. This was, in fact, a topic of discussion among members during the most recent International Symposium. The authors encourage the Board to implement this idea and further expand it to the various committees within the Association.
- A call for student presentations at the International Symposium. This would target student participation and highlight the organization's commitment to this constituency.
- A specific "student-track" composed of a series of workshops aimed at student needs and interests offered at the International Symposium.
- A competition for the best student papers on a group work topic. Awards could be given and papers could be published in the AASWG Newsletter or even in *Social Work with Groups*.
- The designation of student representatives to the local AASWG chapter. Individual chapters could request local colleges and universities to recruit students as official representatives at association meetings.
- The development of scholarships and/or grant opportunities to fund student participation in its Symposia. Perhaps, AASWG could seek earmarked donations or other fundraising opportunities to address increased student participation.

There are many effective methods for connecting students and professional associations. The model presented in this paper is but one. However, if the initial results of this model are an indication of the potential of such endeavors, perhaps the time is right to mount a broad-based, concerted effort to foster the critical relationship between students and professional associations.

Acknowledgement

This article has been published in *Social Work With Groups,* Copyright © 2007 Taylor & Francis Group, LLC. *Social Work With Groups* is available online at: http://www.informaworld.com/WSWG. This article is available online at: http://www.informaworld.com/openurl?genre=article&issn=01609513&volume=30&issue=4&spage=5

References

Bergart, A. & Simon, S. (2004). Practicing what we preach: Creating groups for ourselves. *Social Work with Groups,* 27(4), 17-30.

Birnbaum, M., & Auerbach, C. (1994). Group work in graduate social work education: The price of neglect. *Journal of Social Work Education,* 30(3), 325-335.

Bloome, D., & Harste, J. (2001). Teaching, learning and growing as a member of a professional education community. *Language Arts,* 79(1), 38-39.

Desmond, S., & Symens, A. (1997). Promoting graduate students' membership in professional organizations. *Teaching Sociology,* 25(2), 176-182.

Drumm, K. (2006). The essential power of group work. *Social Work with Groups,* 29(2-3), 17- 31.

Eitzen, D. (1988). The introduction of graduate students to the profession of sociology. *Teaching Sociology,* 16, 279-283.

Gonzales, R. & Scarcella, J. (2001). Welcome, technology educators! *Tech Directions,* 61(5), 19-23.

Goodman, H. & Munoz, M. (2004). Developing social group work skills for contemporary agency practice. *Social Work with Groups,* 27(1), 17-33.

Knight, G. (2002). Never too soon: Music ed students at professional conferences. *Teaching Music,* 9(5), 46-50.

Koch, W., & Sancier, B. (1988). Continuing education for school social workers: A learner- friendly model. *Social Work in Education,* 10(2), 122-132.

Kurland, R., & Salmon, R. (2002). *Caught in the doorway between education and practice: Group work's battle for survival.* Plenary Presentation at the XXIV Annual Symposium of the Association for the Advancement of Social Work with Groups, Boston, MA.

Messmer, M. (2005). Counting the benefits of association involvement. *Strategic Finance,* 87(1), 12-14.

Middleman, R. (1990). Group work and the Heimlich maneuver: Unchoking social work education. In D.F. Fike and B. Rittner (Eds.), *Working from Strengths: The Essence of Group Work.* Miami: Center for Group Work Studies, 16-39.

Putnam, R. (2000). *Bowling Alone: The collapse and revival of American community.* New York: Simon and Schuster.

Royce, C. & Hectman, J. (2001). Forces at work: The top five reasons for belonging to a professional organization. *Science Scope,* 24(6), 28-31.

Schwartz, W. (1974). The social worker in the group. In R. Klenk & R. Ryan (Eds.), *The Practice of Social Work,* (pp. 257-276). CA: Wadsworth Publishing.

Sullivan, N. (2006) From the President's pen: Why belong to AASWG? *Social Work with Groups Newsletter,* 22(59), 1-2,10.

Index

Rutgers University Center 42, 43
Rwandans 139–40

S
sadness 59, 61
  see also crying; grief
Salmon, R. 14–15, 19–20, 21, 24, 25, 31, 46, 149, 151–2
sanctions, and Managing Difficult Behaviour (MDB) groups 74, 80
Sands, R.G. 28
scanning skills 56, 59, 64
Scarcella, J. 149, 150, 151
Scheflen, A. 97
Schein, E.H. 119
schizophrenia patients 119
Schön, D.A. 7
Schopler, J. 55, 56, 65, 67, 68, 119
Schwartz, W. 31, 46–7, 50
Scisney-Matlock, M. 27, 32, 33–4
Scotland *see* group services for older-hearing impaired people
screening 58–62, 74, 124
  see also pre-group interviews; pre-group questionnaires; referrals
seeing 65, 66–8
  see also looking
seeing sound 67–8
self-care, and Managing Difficult Behaviour (MDB) groups 80–1
self-confidence 155
self-esteem 33, 80–1, 87, 132
semi-structured interviews 108–9
September 11, 2001 terrorist attack 139
service user involvement in design of services 112–13
settlement house movement, and group mentoring 28
sexual assault survivors 121
  see also participatory research and evidence-based practice for rape
    survivor groups
sexuality 9–13, 141, 142
Shapiro, B. 42
shared beliefs 19, 24
shared educational background 19, 21, 24, 25
shared engagement 100, 101–2
shared experiences
  group mentoring 28, 35
  group services for older-hearing impaired people 111
  group work for genocide survivors 139–40

Lightning Source UK Ltd.
Milton Keynes UK

177690UK00002B/2/P